Advancing Your Career

Getting and Making the Most of
Your Doctorate

Advancing Your Career

Getting and Making the Most of Your Doctorate

Michael D. Brubaker and Dale L. Brubaker

Nov. 12, 2012

With appreciation and respect for your leadership and fine work.

Dale

ROWMAN & LITTLEFIELD EDUCATION

A division of

ROWMAN & LITTLEFIELD PUBLISHERS, INC.
Lanham • New York • Toronto • Plymouth, UK

Published by Rowman & Littlefield Education
A division of Rowman & Littlefield Publishers, Inc.
A wholly owned subsidary of The Rowman & Littlefield Publishing Group, Inc.
4501 Forbes Boulevard, Suite 200, Lanham, Maryland 20706
http://www.rowmaneducation.com

Estover Road, Plymouth PL6 7PY, United Kingdom

British Library Cataloguing in Publication Information Available

Library of Congress Cataloging-in-Publication Data

Brubaker, Michael D, 1958–
  Advancing your career : getting and making the most of your doctorate / Michael D.
Brubaker and Dale L. Brubaker.
    p. cm.
  Summary: "Advancing Your Career aims to help readers look more broadly at
the doctoral experience from choosing a program to coursework to passing your
comprehensive exams to doing dissertation research and writing to graduation and
beyond."—Provided by publisher.
  Includes biographical references and index.
  ISBN 978-1-61048-490-9 (hardback)—ISBN 978-1-60148-491-6 (paper)—
ISBN 978-1-61048-492-3 (electronic)
  1. Doctor of philosophy degree.   I. Brubaker, Dale L.   II. Title.
  LB2386.B78 2011
  378.2—dc23
                                                                    2011016667

∞™ The paper used in this publication meets the minimum requirements of American
National Standard for Information Sciences—Permanence of Paper for Printed Library
Materials, ANSI/NISO Z39.48-1992.

Printed in the United States of America

Dedication

For doctoral students – past, present, and future
and
the memory of Seymour B. Sarason – professor, mentor, and friend

Contents

Preface

A pre-publication reviewer of this book, who was considering doctoral study, shared with us his major professor's response to this interest: *"Why do you want the degree?"* This question, according to the prospective doctoral student caused a few sleepless nights during which he realized how important the answer to that question was!

Starting a doctoral program can be both an exciting and a daunting experience. Exploring new possibilities for career advancement, envisioning a new life with better pay, more flexibility, and more professional credibility are all enticements to continue along the degree path towards the doctorate. For many, there is a certain feeling about attaining this pinnacle of all degrees, achieving the highest level of success, and being publicly recognized for it. Even at the announcement of your intent to seek this degree, friends, family, and colleagues may begin to call you "doctor" and share a smile as if it were already done.

While there are many reasons to get a doctorate, there are also many challenges that lie ahead. When less than two-thirds of all doctoral students will actually receive their degree (Council of Graduate Schools, 2008; Nettles & Millett, 2006), it can appear that you are beginning to play the roulette table instead of relying on the standard learning tools to earn what is rightfully yours. The doctorate degree is unlike most other degrees, and not all are well prepared to reach the finish line, much less to take full advantage of this opportunity.

If you have gotten to the point where you are considering a doctorate, or you are even well along your way in a program, it is likely that your major focus is trying to write that "little paper," the dissertation. Although this is one of the major hurdles in a doctoral program, there is far less attention paid to the whole doctoral experience, much of which is designed to prepare you to write the dissertation, but even more so, to prepare you for a successful career upon graduation.

The purpose of this book is to look more broadly at the doctoral experience, beginning at the time when one is seriously considering the degree through the first steps in one's new career with doctorate in hand. Throughout this process, there are many stated guidelines, but there are also many unstated rules of the game that are often not revealed until it is too late. Furthermore, over the years, both public and private institutions have dedicated large sums of money and resources to determine the key factors that enhance your chance of successful completion. It is our intent to provide both an insider's look at the process as well as the hard research to better ensure that you realize your dream.

AUDIENCE

This book is designed to be a resource for those who are considering the doctoral degree as well as those who are in various stages of their doctoral program. It is our belief that we must attend to the dream that has inspired us to continue our education and pursue this goal. Nurturing that dream and maintaining support will be an essential ingredient from beginning to end.

Those in the early stages, who are considering the degree, will find the book especially useful as they are weighing the benefits with the costs of continuing their education for the next few years. These readers will have a chance to evaluate their own strengths and limitations while identifying the important aspects of prospective programs to see where there is a good fit. Those who have already begun their journey, having entered a doctoral program, will benefit through this reflective process as well. As readers continue through the book, they will see important meta-perspectives as well as the individual tips to successful completion of the degree.

Professors who are teaching doctoral classes, particularly those courses which serve to orient students to their program, will find this book to be a helpful guide to lead students through an overview of the doctoral process. It is not intended to supplant any program information; rather, it provides a core upon which one may add materials and handbooks in order to more fully engage students. The appendixes are especially useful in this regard. Likewise, university, school, and program administrators will be able to reflect upon their own doctoral programs identifying where students may receive greater support thereby increasing the likelihood of success and productivity.

With regard to the matter of audience, we have been happily surprised by the number of doctoral students outside of schools of education that have found our writings on doctoral studies useful. Seminaries that offer the doctorate of ministry and theological doctorate degree are a case in point as are Ph.D. programs in the social sciences, such as anthropology, sociology, and political science.

Nursing schools and schools of social work that offer doctorates have also adopted our writings for their students. Our invitation to e-mail us with a promised response at the end of this preface is an invitation to keep us up-to-date on who is using the book. Previous invitations in other books and references to them on search engines have yielded responses from around our nation and indeed the world.

WHAT IS UNIQUE ABOUT THIS BOOK?

Unlike books that only focus on dissertation research and writing, this book takes you through all of the stages of the doctoral journey from imagining yourself as a doctoral student *to* assessing yourself as a potential doctoral candidate *to* applying to one or more doctoral programs *to* program planning *to* internships, assistantships and fellowships *to* comprehensive examinations *to* dissertation research and writing *to* graduation and beyond.

Importantly, the book gives specific and concrete advice about how to maintain your momentum from one stage to the next, fending off those external and internal obstacles that may get you stuck and may prevent you from finishing the degree. The goal is a seamless doctoral program.

Two important perspectives will guide you on this journey. The first author received his doctorate more recently, giving him a current first-hand understanding of the student perspective and witnessing the trends in doctoral education, such as the use of research technology, online pedagogy and successful negotiation of an increasingly competitive job market. The second author has over four decades of experience in advising doctoral students in four different universities.

Both of the authors draw on their own experiences as a student, colleague, and mentor, presenting "snapshots"—brief sketches that illustrate key points. The topics discussed herein are important, but the real impact of these issues is brought to life when a personal face is placed on them. Snapshots tell the stories that take you, the reader, backstage into the lives of doctoral students and those who influence them. These personal anecdotes show an often humorous look at the inner workings of programs and the dialogue shared between students and faculty. Some of these snapshots are descriptions of what we have experienced in our own lives and what others have shared with us. Others are composites.

It will be helpful to imagine this book as an ongoing conversation you are having with two faculty members, the authors, who are interested in your personal success. As such, we will each address you throughout the book in the second person. With a clear and understandable voice, our aim is to stimulate thought and discussion among you, prospective doctoral candidates, doctoral students, professors, and others who have a stake in your success.

Epigraphs (header quotes) introduce each chapter, thus setting the tone for the writing that follows. These quotes may be useful in doctoral students' dissertation writing as will be numerous references to important research and writing in the book.

Many of you will find the interactive appendixes at the end of the book personally useful as you read the book. We encourage you to talk about your discoveries with those who are part of your support network. Often, these are the people who can provide honest feedback and serve as a general sounding board. Others, such as dissertation seminar professors and those who teach introductory doctoral-level courses, can use the appendixes as instructional tools. These courses are often designed to help orient students to doctoral programs. References to appropriate appendixes will be made throughout the book.

Finally, the thesis of this book is that your relationships with others and the work itself during the doctoral program will be the key to your success. The learning you will experience during this defining moment in your career and life will depend in large measure on the steps you take to connect with a number of people: program advisor, professors at your university and at other universities, fellow students, intern advisor, dissertation advisor, and dissertation committee members.

Your learning will also center on your evaluation of the work you do as a scholar in general and researcher and writer in particular. (See appendix A, Bringing Coherence to the Body of Work You've Done in Preparation for Doctoral Study.) Reid Buckley says with great insight in his book, *This Business of Writing . . . Wresting Order Out of Chaos* (2010): "On balance, will the good, the true, and the beautiful be served by what I have done? You also must draw the final judgment of your work, no one else" (p. 67).

ORGANIZATION OF THE BOOK

We have identified three stages to consider in order to maximize your attainment and use of your doctorate. Stage I, "Preparing the Way," is the planning stage, that time before entering a doctoral program when the dream emerges and you begin to seriously explore your options. Chapter 1, "Following Your Dream: An Assessment of Self and Your Resources," attends to the power of this dream and how it finds root in the present realities of your current situation. From a practical standpoint, this chapter provides you an excellent opportunity to assess yourself and your support network before you start looking at particular programs. This will be a chance for you to explore the question, *Is a doctorate right for me?*

Chapter 2, "Applying to a Doctoral Program," focuses on the other perspective of this matchmaking endeavor, that of the doctoral program. Just as with any organization, each program is unique, and should be interviewed, just as you will be. Once you identify the best program(s) for you, this chapter will offer some practical tips on how to present yourself and secure a position.

Stage II, "How to Thrive in Your Doctoral Program," begins once you enter the doctoral program. While some talk of the doctorate as a matter of endurance and survival, we see it as a place where you may thrive. In chapter 3, "Composing Inner Curriculum and Influencing Outer Curriculum in Doctoral Study," we discuss important considerations facing you when relating to the program's outer curriculum and composing your inner curriculum. While one of your key requirements will be to propose a formal course of study, many forget to attend to the inner, hidden curriculum, which is a driving force and is rooted in the dream that brought you to this place. By carefully choosing your advisor and assembling your program committee members, you will be able to attend to both the inner curriculum and the outer curriculum.

While determining your planned program, there are many experiences beyond the coursework to pay careful attention to as they can support your overall goals or become time-consuming distractions. In chapter 4, "Obtaining and Maintaining Graduate Assistantships and Internships," we discuss the opportunities and pitfalls that may occur in internships, assistantships, and fellowships in doctoral studies. With your vision for the future as a guide, we will identify how to best use these experiences to your advantage.

Chapter 5, "Comprehensive Examinations," focuses on this important challenge. For some this is more of a millstone around the neck than a milestone of achievement. We offer some advice on the timing and use of these exams to not only pass, but to sustain your momentum as you prepare for the dissertation.

The final milestone, the dissertation, is discussed in chapter 6, "Researching and Writing the Dissertation." The chapter will show how thoughtful planning in the early stages of the doctoral program will set you up for the successful completion of the dissertation. It will summarize the essential components of dissertation planning, research, and writing. This chapter is extensive and has been reviewed favorably by professors who teach dissertation seminars.

Stage III, "Graduation and Beyond: The Difference You Can Make Now That You Have a Doctorate," begins at graduation and continues into the early phases of one's next professional steps. Chapter 7, "Reaching a Wider Audience," provides guidance on how to reach a wider audience with your writing and speaking now that you have earned the doctorate. No one wants to be called Doctor Doolittle. Indeed, there are many opportunities for you to share your research and talents in a variety of communities and enjoy the fruits of your labor.

References and an index conclude the book. In the conversational spirit of this book, we urge you to write us at our e-mail addresses so that we can converse with each other: michael.brubaker@uc.edu and dlbrubak@uncg.edu. We promise a response.

Acknowledgments

Our special appreciation and thanks go to the doctoral students and graduates who shared stories about what they experienced when going through their programs. Our colleagues and friends were also helpful in this regard. Thank you also to the many mentors who showed us the power of living our inner curriculum each and every day.

All authors know the importance of excellent editors and production staff. It does indeed take a community to give birth to a book. We especially want to thank Thomas F. Koerner, Ph.D., vice president and editorial director, Rowman & Littlefield Education, and Lindsey Schauer, assistant editor, who showed us every courtesy authors could want.

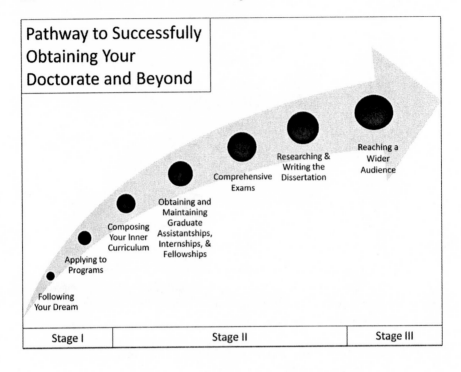

Pathway to Successfully Obtaining Your Doctorate and Beyond

Following Your Dream

Applying to Programs

Composing Your Inner Curriculum

Obtaining and Maintaining Graduate Assistantships, Internships, & Fellowships

Comprehensive Exams

Researching & Writing the Dissertation

Reaching a Wider Audience

Stage I

Stage II

Stage III

Stage I

Preparing the Way

Preparing the way to begin doctoral study means that you are making yourself ready or positioning yourself by combining helpful information, skills and attitudes. Imagining yourself with a doctorate is a natural first step in this process. What would it sound like to have the title of Dr. in front of my name? Chapter 1, "Following Your Dream: An Assessment of Self," makes it clear that self-assessment provides the context for your decision to either pursue the doctorate or not.

We note in chapter 1 the role of influential persons and events in fueling the dream. We then turn to the challenge of balancing the dream with present realities. What forces work in your favor to pursue the dream and what forces serve as internal and external barriers? What does your track record say about how you might do in a doctoral program?

Entrance examinations and the like are also discussed in chapter 1. A series of important questions need to be asked: How do I define success and what role would my entering a doctoral program play in this regard? Why should I apply for a doctoral program? How sure am I about this decision? Finally, what advantages are there to my pursuing the doctorate?

Chapter 2, "Applying to a Doctoral Program," speaks to the matter of choosing a program. Recognizing that there are many ways to achieve the dream of earning a doctorate, what path is best for me to follow? In particular, what doctoral degree should I pursue given my interests and talents? Geographical location of the program and the university in which it resides are other issues to be addressed. Where do I want to go? What resources do I have and need to go where I want to go? Possible scholarship and fellowship opportunities are also a consideration.

What is the quality of the faculty at the university that interests me? Is there a fixed number of openings in the program for admission? What are the possibilities of working with a person or persons I have identified as experts in this university? What opportunities will I have in the application process to demonstrate my talents and academic successes from the past? It is our purpose to help you sort out these and other related issues for your consideration.

Chapter 1

Following Your Dream

An Assessment of Self and Your Resources

Being in the master's program helped me investigate the kind of mentor I wanted in the doctoral program. Developmentally, I wanted and needed a lot of guidance and reassurance. To feel supported I needed someone I liked being around, a person who was a lot of fun. It was mutual. That translated into wanting to do work together.

—Rachel Goodman (2010)

Hope resides in the future, while perspective and wisdom are almost always found by looking to the past.

—Greg Mortenson (2009, p. 21)

Memory is not meant to cement us in times past. It is meant to enable us to do better now that which we did not do as well before. It is the greatest teacher of them all. In our dreams lies our unfinished work for the world.

—Joan Chittister (2008, pp. 136 & 156)

Many of the important trips we took as children began as a dream of what it would be like to reach our destination. Can you hear children in the back seat of the car saying "How long? How long 'til we get there?" This dream "has the quality of a vision, an imagined possibility that generates excitement and vitality" (Levinson, 1985, p. 91). Think back to your first trip to Disney World or Disneyland. As one wag said, "Half the fun is dreaming about the place before you get there."

THE POWER OF THE DREAM

Actually beginning a doctoral program is preceded by imagining that you have the degree or what we call the power of the dream. Yet, strangely enough, this factor of the power of the dream "often portrayed in mythology and literature, is rarely considered in academic research" (Levinson, 1985, p. 91). The late Daniel Levinson, Professor of Psychology in the Department of Psychiatry of the Yale School of Medicine, adds that "a 'dream' of this kind is more formed than a pure fantasy, yet less articulated than a fully thought-out plan" (1985, p. 91).

"Why should I get a doctorate?" is a question that can lead to many different answers, some of which are clearly known and others that are not. There are times when a person interested in earning a doctorate sees this dream as part of occupational advancement, but there are other times when the dream is less concrete due to the fact that you have already reached the ceiling in your profession or you simply don't want to pursue a higher professional level. Age and family responsibilities may be considerations. Some prospective students simply love learning and are not sure where seeking and getting the degree will lead them.

The fact is, however, that the dream does connote responsibilities. "The holder of the dream has the developmental task of giving it greater definition and finding ways to live it out" (Levinson, 1985, p. 91). You have to have a plan and work the plan.

The following snapshot brings life to what we have said thus far regarding the role of the dream in beginning the doctoral program journey.

Snapshot 1.1

The Power of a Dream

A friend of mine who was in my master's program was excited about working on a doctorate and invited me to go with her to a recruiting session for interested persons at a nearby university. I wasn't sure I had the right stuff to be a doctoral student, but I decided to go with her to investigate the doctoral program.

Two presenters, the director of the doctoral program and a recent doctoral graduate, were there along with nearly thirty persons interested in doctoral study. The director gave what I considered a rather dry talk citing facts and figures, after which he handed out a brochure and application forms.

The recent graduate of the program introduced reality into the presentation by telling stories. She said that four years ago she had been sitting where we were now sitting listening to a description of the program. She shared with us that she had reservations about the program and her ability to complete it, but she took the plunge because she had a dream about what it would be like to have Doctor in front of her name. She imagined herself being introduced as a well-known speaker with important things to say to an audience of interested people.

She proceeded to tell us that during her first doctoral level course her professor gave each student a five by seven card and asked the students to make a horizontal fold midway down the card. The students were directed to put the folded card on the desk in front of them so that it looked like a tent. Each person's name was to be written on both sides of the card, one without Doctor in front of it, the other with Dr. in front of it. The name with Dr. on it would face the students throughout the course to remind them of the importance of graduating with a doctorate in hand.

The recent doctoral graduate and recruiter continued by saying that this beginning exercise in her first class was not only a good way to get to know other students but more importantly to keep the vision of having a doctorate in front of her throughout the program.

She concluded her presentation with a kind of warning to us. She said she was changed during the doctoral program in ways that she had not anticipated, and the degree opened doors for her that led to new responsibilities and challenges. She didn't elaborate, but we sensed that she was a different person, at least to some extent, because she followed her dream and reached her goal of receiving a doctorate.

All of this is by way of saying that there is power in having and realizing the dream. "The vicissitudes and fate of the Dream have fundamental consequences for adult development" (Levinson, 1978, p. 91). It is one of a few times in your life that you get a fresh start. When you are first addressed as Doctor you will hardly believe it. (See appendix B, "Selecting a Doctoral Program.")

INFLUENTIAL PERSONS AND EVENTS
THAT FUEL THE DREAM

The holder of the dream "must form significant relationships with other adults who will facilitate work on the dream" (Levinson, 1978, p. 93). Mentors, other professors and experts, family and friends can play important roles in fueling your dream of earning a doctorate.

Mentors

A mentor can be especially helpful in enhancing your skills and intellectual development. The mentor can introduce you to a new social and occupational world with its own symbols, customs, value system, and leading figures. The mentor can also be a role model, an exemplar that you can emulate. Occasionally a person being mentored will have a slip of the tongue and address the mentor as mother or father. (See Shapiro, 2010, p. 319). In the emotion of the moment the mentor can easily be identified as having mother- or father-like qualities. But, the most important function the mentor has "is developmentally the most crucial one: to support and facilitate the *realization of the Dream*" (Levinson, 1978, p. 98).

As you think about the role mentors have played in fueling your dream of entering and completing a doctoral program, we would like to have you consider the following ideas about mentoring in an award winning article, *"We're Not Just Interested in the Work": Social and Emotional Aspects of Early Educator Mentoring Relations,* by Shira M. Peterson, Constance Valk, Amy C. Baker, Lauri Brugger and A. Dirk Hightower (2010, pp. 155–175).

- Mentoring is a one-on-one long-term relationship between an expert and a novice that supports your professional, academic and personal development.
- Mentors have a genuine interest in you as a person and are not simply interested in your work.
- Mentors integrate three functions in your learning relationship—offering support, creating a challenge, and facilitating a professional vision.
- The role mentors play is often ambiguous.
- Mentors try to build up your confidence to succeed.

It is interesting to see how these factors play out in the following comments by graduate students:

- A professor in my master's program, George Axtelle, a visiting summer-school professor from New York University, wrote a letter to the dean of the college at the university with a copy to me saying that I was precisely the kind of student who should be in the doctoral program. The dean asked me to make an appointment with him, which I did, and we had a conversation in which I was assured admission to the doctoral program. The traditional entrance procedures were largely bypassed. This was the beginning of Dr. Axtelle's mentoring of me even though he was at another university most of the time.

- I was nearly at the end of my master's program and thought that I was just another student in a class taught by a professor I respected for creativity and intelligence. I wrote a paper that I really enjoyed doing the research for, and this professor wrote at the end of the paper, "You have what it takes to be a student in our doctoral program." I knew at this moment that I would apply for doctoral study. This professor became a mentor for me even though I never addressed the professor with this title.
- I met with the professor in charge of admissions to the doctoral program and said that I thought I was too old to get into the program in spite of my excellent grades and leadership experience in schools. The professor said, "You're probably right." I was so mad that I applied anyway and got into the program. I talked to this professor after getting my acceptance letter. He said: "I wanted you in the program but said what I did in order to get you off the dime to make a commitment and get on with things." We both laughed. He became my advisor and mentor, and I went on to have a very successful career as an educational leader for another decade or so before I retired. I then served several terms as a school board member in a large school system.
- I was cocky and didn't think I needed a doctorate but decided anyway to make an appointment with the director of the doctoral program to discuss the program. The director invited me to lunch. I began the conversation by listing all of the things I knew and said that I really didn't need a doctorate, thinking that he would try to talk me into applying for the program. The director called my bluff and said, "You're right. You already know and have everything you need. You don't need a doctorate!"

  I was angry at the director at the time but realized after thinking about it that I didn't deserve to be in the program at that time. I needed an attitude adjustment. A couple of years later I met with the director again, apologized for my earlier attitude and made the case for myself as a more mature student. I got in the program, worked hard, and became a research assistant under the director who in the process became my mentor.

It is interesting with the previous comments how many twists and turns there can be in a relationship between student and professor leading to a mentorship of value to both of them. Our own experience has taught us that there is no formula or perfect set of guidelines that those who administer doctoral programs, professors and students should follow in relating to each other. Authenticity, respect, sensitivity and good will seem to be the most important factors in these relationships.

Some of you will have one or more mentors already in place when you begin your doctoral program. You may add other mentors as you move forward in the program. Some of you may begin doctoral study without knowing any professors. The mentoring process is interesting in that you will need to assume a proactive role in establishing relationships with mentors.

Other Professors and Experts

One of the fascinating things about the dream of getting a doctorate is that you are often surprised how a brief encounter with a professor or expert in a topic or field of study can fuel your dream. (See appendix H, "Identifying the Traits of Outstanding Leaders Encountered During My Doctoral Program.") Students shared the following examples of this with us.

- I was a high school social studies teacher when I heard a speaker at the fall orientation session for faculty, staff, and administrators in the school system. The superintendent of schools, who was also a doctoral student at a nearby university, invited a keynote speaker who addressed us on Soviet Education.

  The guest, a professor at Teachers College, Columbia University, was an expert on this subject, one that interested me as I had a course in it in my master's program and was seriously considering pursuing the topic in a doctoral program. I'm not sure if this speech spoke to others, but I was mesmerized by it to the extent that I knew I would do more with this topic in a doctoral program. A brief conversation with the speaker after this event further reinforced my interest in the subject.
- The dynamics of my master's program intrigued me, especially since we were a cohort of approximately twenty students who took the same courses together over the course of a year and really got to know each other well. There were a few serious scholars in our cohort along with others who seemed to want to simply jump over the hurdles in order to get the degree. These students sometimes joked about the vocabularies being developed by those of us who took the program seriously. We would use a new word we learned, such as "critique" or "hermeneutics," and they would roll their eyes and smile.

  I appreciated the fact that the professor in charge of the master's program gave special attention to, in fact seemed to groom, those of us identified as potential doctoral program students. For example, we were urged to apply for stipends that would let us attend a conference in our area of study in New Orleans. I did this, attended the conference, and decided to apply for the doctoral program upon graduation from the master's program. I was given the message by this experience that I had the right stuff to earn a doctorate.
- Two parents of students in the high school where I taught, one a professor in the discipline that I was interested in getting a doctorate in and another a school board member and wife of a professor at the university where I

wanted to get my doctorate, were very supportive of my interest in doctoral study. I gave the school board member a copy of my master's thesis, and she responded with high praise and the recommendation that I try to get part or all of it published. The professor in the discipline I was interested in was most supportive and wrote a letter of recommendation to the doctoral entrance committee. He eventually became my advisor.

These statements by aspiring doctoral students illustrate how you might consider the variety of contacts you presently have or could create in order to fuel the dream you have to enter and/or complete your doctoral program. Once again, your making the effort to let potential supporters know what your dream is with regard to doctoral study is the key to opening this door.

Family and Friends

Our discussions with doctoral students have revealed a surprising number of different responses with respect to how family and friends fueled their dream of entering and completing a doctoral program. You will see from the following statements from doctoral students that seemingly negative comments from parents and friends sometimes fueled the dream as much or more than completely positive statements.

- My mother was a teacher who loved learning and encouraged me each step of the way from kindergarten through my master's program. When I told her I was considering pursuing a doctorate she said that she would support me in any way that she could and she did. In fact, she gave me a cap and gown when I began work on the dissertation as an incentive to complete the doctorate and walk across the stage at graduation.
- My father said that I should not go straight from my master's program into a doctoral program but should instead go into the work world for a few years in spite of my strong interest in continuing doctoral study. He wanted me to meet with a friend of his who was a college president and shared his view on this matter. He also said that I would lose the financial security I needed by pushing forward after the master's degree.

  I knew that he was conservative on such matters and always advised me to play it safe. His being against my dream convinced me that I should immediately apply for the doctoral program as I had an advisor in place from my master's degree who promised me a research assistantship. Also, my spouse had no reservations about supporting me in this venture.
- A friend and I were principals in the same school system and got our master's degrees together. We studied together, read each other's papers

and encouraged each other each step of the way. We knew we wanted
to become superintendents of schools and needed doctorates in order to
get good school systems. We therefore applied for doctoral study at the
same time, got in the program and supported each other right up through
graduation. Professors sometimes kidded us that we were joined together
at the hip.

- Several of my colleagues in the high school where I taught left me with the
feeling that they thought I was better than they were by being interested in
getting into the doctoral program. They were quite a bit older than I was,
and I thought there was some jealousy involved in their discouraging comments. In some strange way their comments motivated me all the more to
pursue my dream of getting a doctorate.

- I was a master's student in a very large program in a university that had
nearly forty thousand students. My advisor, who also was my professor
in two large classes, met with me two to three times during the master's
program. I earned two excellent grades in these classes. My advisor didn't
return my call when I left a message saying I was interested in doctoral
study. When I talked with the secretary she said that the professor said that
he didn't know me. This bureaucratic response was irritating, and yet it
spurred me on to enter and complete a doctorate in another university.

- At the non-profit where I worked, I had a volunteer who always came up
to me, calling me Dr. Schieble. He learned that I was interested in the degree, but was still unsure about it. There was something about the way he
held me in such high esteem when he bestowed this degree upon me, even
though I clearly knew I had not earned it. It was as if he saw something in
me that I could not see in myself.

- While sitting in my group counseling class one day, my peers asked me if I
had ever thought of getting a doctorate degree. "Not really," I offered, knowing that I really wanted to be a clinician. "You really have a way of describing difficult concepts," they told me. Then a professor described to me how
she could impact so many more lives through her teaching, it dawned on me
that I could be an effective clinician and professor, all in one.

The variety of responses that fueled the dream of entering and completing a doctoral program demonstrate how your belief in yourself and your
definition of success are central to your mission. You will reach your goal
in some way in some place if you have the determination to move forward.
It will be up to you to create and maintain a core group of support. You
would not be in the place you are now in life if you didn't have the right
stuff to do this.

ASSESSING YOUR TRACK RECORD

It is important before applying to a doctoral program, the subject of chapter 2, that you assess your track record in order to put your best face forward. We will speak to this matter by discussing seven factors: the prestige of the institutions you have already attended; your majors and minors and their prestige; your grade point averages; the strength of recommendations; previous research and writing; career and work experiences; and scores on entrance examinations. All must be considered in total, for if one area is weaker for you, it will be important to emphasize your other strengths and identify a range of programs where you may be competitive.

Prestige of Institutions Already Attended

Prestige is an interesting word and concept. Webster's Dictionary (2002) reads as follows: "1. the power to impress or influence, 2. reputation based on high achievement, character, etc." (p. 382). The prestige of your undergraduate institution will be viewed within the context of the state, the region and the nation. The same thing is also true for the master's degree that most of you will have before pursuing a doctorate.

It will not surprise you if you read descriptions of colleges and universities that they all claim to be prestigious. The same thing is true if you search online under "prestige" and "institutions of higher education."

People involved in doctoral program admissions will make public statements about the prestige of institutions you have attended: "That's a first-rate or excellent university." "That's a good school." This is especially true if they attended these institutions of higher education. They are reluctant and wise not to voice their judgments about colleges and universities they think are inferior.

It has been our experience that professors and administrators involved in doctoral program student admissions will make public statements of a judgmental nature to fellow members of admissions committees about colleges and universities that they think are quite good and quite poor and say little if anything about institutions of higher education that are between these two extremes.

These judgments are based on where they got their degrees, the scholarship or lack of scholarship on the part of students they have taught and folklore shared by others with them. As members of these doctoral admissions committees we have not heard direct references to rankings of an applicants' colleges and universities by *U.S. News and World Report*, the *National Research Council,* and the like. However, we should note that these rankings can influence the general opinion of the institution(s) that you have attended.

If you wish to read more on this subject, we recommend an article by historian Hugh Davis Graham titled *Should We Abolish Ranking Universities by Their Reputations?* (2000, pp. 1–5). He argues that rising challengers, those universities with smaller faculties and student bodies, are at a disadvantage with regard to rankings based on prestige because "reputational surveys are biased toward size, as larger programs often benefit not only from a greater number of visible publishing researchers, but also from a greater number of graduates doing the rating" (p. 1).[1]

If you find yourself in one of these programs that are underrecognized in comparison to other larger programs, do not be discouraged. When applying to programs, you have the ability to stress your individual strengths and experiences as well as those of your latest program and noteworthy mentors. We will address each of these next.

Majors and Minors and their Prestige

Your major and minor as an undergraduate are of interest but usually less important to doctoral admissions committees than your major and perhaps minor in your master's program. It is in the master's program that your focus is clearer and you demonstrate research and writing skills more like those expected in doctoral study.

If you wrote a thesis in your master's program, it is evidence of your ability to complete a significant research and writing project. Doctoral admissions committees also give attention to your competence as a quantitative and qualitative researcher as demonstrated in courses in these subjects in your master's program.

If your major in your master's program is also the major you wish to pursue in the doctoral program, the reputation or prestige of your master's major can be important. Doctoral admissions committee members will want to know who you worked with, the extent of your research and writing in the master's major and the quality of this work. It is frequently the case that professors in a prestigious doctoral program will have earned their doctorates in other high prestige doctoral programs in the nation and know other prominent professors who have taught and mentored you. This is one of the reasons why prestigious programs continue to remain in that category. "Reputational surveys . . . benefit from a greater number of graduates doing the rating" (Graham, 2000, p. 1).

All of these matters should be considered by you as you assess your master's degree program and your track record from your master's degree program in preparation for your making the case for yourself when you apply for a doctoral program. It will be especially important that you can articulate your track record in an interview situation.

Grade Point Averages

The rule of thumb for doctoral entrance committee members is to give close attention to the grades you earned in courses you took during the last two years of your undergraduate degree and your master's degree with special attention given to the latter. This is the case since during this period of time you attended courses in your major that really mattered to you.

Grade inflation in master's programs is expected, with anything lower than a B standing out on a transcript. You should be prepared to explain this lower grade in an interview situation. It is not unusual to see a master's transcript with a 3.5 GPA or higher. It has been our experience that high or low grades in statistics during a master's program are often discussed by doctoral entrance committees as a forecast of success or difficulties in more advanced courses in the same area and dissertation research in a doctoral program.

Strength of Possible Recommendations

As you assess the strength of recommendations for doctoral study that you believe you can acquire, you are actually assessing the strength of the professional network you have created. It is our view that the leverage you have as a decision-maker depends on the quality of your professional network. It is this leverage that you have used or will use to enter and complete your doctoral program.

You should be able to identify three or four reputable persons in your network who will give you recommendations that speak to those qualities that will be valued by a doctoral program admissions committee. Your recommendations should highlight your substantive knowledge in the area in which you will do your doctoral study and your attitudes and behaviors as a scholar who will successfully complete the doctoral program. The potential that you developed in your master's program should be spoken to in recommendations for doctoral study.

All recommendations should focus on several, if not all, of the following qualities: taking the initiative; perseverance; follow-through in completing what you start; a good attitude in working with others; leadership; the ability to articulate your ideas, verbally and in writing; and other skills associated with scholarship. Professors, intern advisors, and professionals you worked with during the internship are candidates for writing recommendations. Those who recommend you should cite specific examples of your abilities where possible.

The person you select to write your recommendation ideally will have known you for an extended period of time (2–3 years or more) and can attest to your character and skills through concrete examples. As you seek these letters, it can be helpful to remind your recommenders of these accomplishments and activities that they have witnessed. It is also helpful to know that he or she can write well on your behalf. We have seen many letters written by capable practitioners who simply are not used to or do not have the time to write polished recommendations. Recommendations from those with doctorate degrees in your field of interest are credible in that they understand the general requirements to get the doctorate and can attest to your ability to do the same.

An issue that you should assess directly in your track record and considering work as a doctoral student is your motivation for getting the degree. Some of you will have a position in mind that you want to hold after graduation. Others will simply want to enhance your abilities in your present job. A candidate will sometimes say, "I love learning." We have heard every reason possible from "I want to have the position you now hold as a professor" to "I want to sit in a rocker on my front porch and look at my diploma." We were more impressed with the former response than the latter one.

If you are seeking admission to a doctoral program in the same discipline or area of study in the same university where you earned the master's degree, it is to your advantage to have a professor from that program write a strong letter of support for your candidacy. Doctoral admissions committees are hard-pressed to turn down a colleague who writes a letter of recommendation for a doctoral program applicant and agrees to serve as that student's advisor. The issue of who the student's advisor will be, a matter of resource allocation, is not raised.

Previous Research and Writing

All of you have been engaged in research and writing even though it may have never been published. Many of your master's level papers, although not published, may be considered a form of research (literature review) where you bring new knowledge to the field by synthesizing and critically analyzing the existing literature. If your research that led to writing was published, this is something that a doctoral program admissions committee will want to see. If your work was not published, the committee will still want to know about and perhaps look at those papers that you consider to be your best work. What topics interested you and why? Do you want to do more with them in doctoral study, perhaps even to the extent that you want to consider them for dissertation work?

The admissions committee wants to see vitality and interest in research and writing on your part. They also want to hear that you believe that they and other professors can help you develop this interest in research and writing. What a compliment it is to them to hear this from you. Three young ambitious master's graduates interested in doctoral study traveled together across country to the University of Wisconsin-Milwaukee saying that they wanted to work with professors in the department. Professors were surprised and flattered. The visitors were admitted, made an important contribution to the department, graduated, and became highly successful leaders in higher education.

Professors are always searching for doctoral candidates who will enrich their own research and writing as well as others in their community of scholars. Today's doctoral students are increasingly involved in co-authorships with professors. Some of these students become full-time researchers and writers in public and privately funded projects after graduation. Others continue to research and write with their doctoral program professors when they leave the university from which they graduated. We also note the number of professors who add former doctoral students as co-authors to later editions of successful books. The torch from the senior author is passed on to the next generation.

Career and Work Experiences

It is easy to pass over what you have learned in career and work experiences as you assess your track record. It is a natural tendency to focus on what you hope to achieve in the future. It is sometimes helpful to talk to others about these experiences after asking them to note what they see as possible relationships with what you hope to learn in doctoral study. (See appendix A, "Bringing Coherence to the Body of Work You've Done in Preparation for Doctoral Study.")

A high school teacher talked to a friend's mother, who was a college president, about becoming a history professor. The aspiring doctoral student loved intellectual history of the United States and held a master's degree with honors in history from a Big 10 university. The college president noted during their conversation that the high school teacher had been heavily involved in leadership positions in high school and higher education institutions. For example, she was president of the student council in high school, president of the state social studies organization in undergraduate school, and head of a task force that worked with the state's museum while working on her master's degree.

The college president urged the high school teacher to consider giving attention to higher education administration, perhaps even getting a minor in this area of study as part of her doctoral program in history. She added, "You may even want to be a college or university president some day!"

The college president was actually making the case for higher education's increasing attention to multidisciplinary approaches. As Hugh Davis Graham, Holland N. McTyeire Professor of History and professor of political science at Vanderbilt University, noted, "the boundaries of our academic associations have become more flexible and permeable" (2000, p. 2).

As many doctoral programs are training students to teach new practitioners, they are interested in seeing how you will be able to translate your clinical experience into insightful lessons for the classroom and hard research that you will publish. It is always helpful to articulate experiences that 1) relate directly to the content you may research and teach, 2) demonstrate your ability to communicate effectively in both face-to-face and online classrooms, 3) inspire your possible research focus, and 4) demonstrate your ability to conduct research (i.e., prior research team experience even if not in your discipline).

We urge you to assess your career and work experiences in any way you can, alone and with others, so that you can discover new relationships with what you want to learn and accomplish during doctoral study. When you visit universities with doctoral programs you are interested in, you may well be surprised with the positive response of professors and administrators to the connections you have made between your work and career experiences and their descriptions of doctoral programs.

Finally, with regard to all of the factors we have discussed in assessing your track record, it is never too late to improve your record. We hope that this section of the chapter stimulates you to explore ways to do this.

Entrance Examinations

Entrance examination scores will join the package of materials you send to university officials who are in charge of doctoral program admissions. Undergraduate and master's degree transcripts, letters of recommendation, and your personal statement are already in this package. Entrance exams will not only be considered for admissions but they will also be looked at when you apply for scholarships, fellowships and other kinds of financial aid. The weight given to entrance exams varies from place-to place. You will naturally want to talk to anyone connected with this matter in order to get the inside story.

Scores are considered by organizations and publications that rank programs, disciplines and areas of study thus putting pressure on universities to raise them. Interestingly enough, some universities require these examinations but consider them of little or no importance in the admissions process.

Because of the standardized nature of these exams, they are given significant weight by ratings publications (e.g. *U.S. News and World Report*). Some programs have learned to negotiate this game by allowing standardized test scores to be submitted optionally as supplemental materials. Thus, only the higher scores get submitted, which are then reported to these ratings magazines. In these cases, the score may not be used at all in the admissions decisions.

Many of you are already acquainted with the Graduate Record Exam (GRE), a standardized test created and administered by Educational Testing Service (ETS) in 1949. It purports to measure reasoning, critical thinking, and writing skills. The GRE is divided into three sections: a thirty-question verbal section, a twenty-eight-question quantitative section, and a two-part analytical writing section. Non-graded sections used for research purposes may also be added to the text but will not affect your score.

The GRE is a timed test, and so you should memorize the reading instructions for individual exam sections from a practice test thus saving you time in reading the actual test when you take it. One of the sites offering free online practice tests is http://www.examville.com You can check your score and see the review page with answers and explanations. Points are not deducted for incorrect answers, and so it is wise to make educated guesses.

As with other entrance examinations, the GRE General Test can be taken on the computer at qualified testing centers. Critics of the test argue that it is too rigid to be of value. Racial bias criticisms have also been used against the exam. You will want to check on changes in the examination as changes have taken place nearly every year.

The Miller Analogies Test (MAT) is purported to measure analytic ability. It is published by Harcourt Assessment, Inc. Analogies are inferences that imply similarities. Relationships between concepts, English language facility and general knowledge are tested by the MAT. A hundred and twenty questions are on the exam with a hundred of them counted toward the test score. Your basic knowledge of liberal arts subjects, natural and social sciences and mathematics is tested.

You can prepare by using a MAT Test Study Guide and/or a MAT Test Flashcards. Commonly tested words are on sample exams. After finding out how much time you have to complete each section of the exam you can allocate your time accordingly.

As with the GRE, it is wise to read the instructions for taking the MAT ahead of time If you have any questions about items on the practice exam, be sure to ask them before taking the actual exam. Some students have also advised those preparing to take the MAT to answer those questions you find easiest before moving on to more difficult items. Be sure to pace yourself as you work on each section of the exam. Finally, arrive at the test site with plenty of time and necessary supplies in hand: number 2 pencils, a photo ID card, our admission ticket, clothing that is not obtrusive, a water bottle, a snack, and the like.

It is also wise, as you might imagine, to pace yourself in studying for the MAT. Some students wait until the last minute and cram in an all-nighter. Be wary of advice that some exam takers want to give you on exam day. Stay focused on what you have studied and don't be distracted by other students.

As you might imagine, graduate school testing services are a big business with all the strengths and weaknesses that that implies. We urge you to talk to those who have done well on these examinations in order to get the best advice possible as you move forward with admission to doctoral study processes. (See appendix E, "Dealing with Contradictions in a Doctoral Program.")

---

1. The rapidly changing nature of doctoral programs and the expansion of such programs in universities across the country in the late twentieth century are described by Hugh Davis Graham and Nancy Diamond in *Rise of American Research Universities: Elites and Challengers in the Postwar Era* (1997).

Chapter 2

Applying to a Doctoral Program

The voluntary taking of serious chances is a means for the maintenance and acquisition of character.

—Erving Goffman (1967, p. 238)

Achievement is talent plus preparation.

—Malcolm Gladwell (2008, p. 38)

We owe everything to human creativity. Everything that lasts, that changes our lives, that emerges from what was once unimaginable has its roots in that initial spark of innovation.

—Joshua Cooper Ramo (2009, p. 240)

Your self-assessment in chapter 1 was in preparation for actually applying to one or more doctoral programs. (See appendix B, "Selecting a Doctoral Program.") Some of you are extremely mobile and may want to apply to a program far from home. Many of you are somewhat place-bound at this time and will be limited to doctoral programs within driving distance. And still others will apply for programs that are largely, if not entirely, online. Among those in this latter category are those of you who will join a cohort of doctoral students within driving distance who meet monthly and also do a good deal of online work. Your instructors may meet with you for some classes, and your site administrator will meet with you each month or so.

All of these options make it clear that there are many ways to reach your dream of getting a doctorate that will open doors for you to learn new things and give you new employment opportunities. We are all wise at this point to remind ourselves of the subtitle of this book, *Getting and Making the Most of Your Doctorate*. The doctoral program that you choose to apply to should help you build relationships that will bring out the best in you as a learner and leader and at the same time help create networks that will open up career opportunities.

It is also true that the specific goal you have with regard to a particular career emphasis may change as you go through your doctoral program. In fact, a rich and varied doctoral program should introduce you to career possibilities that you may never have thought of when you began your program. For example, a doctoral student in a counseling program changed her major focus from counseling in the private sector to counseling in a not-for-profit organization that helped survivors of family violence. Another student was interested in becoming a high level administrator in public school systems but instead decided to become a professor with special emphasis on leadership education.

The point of all of this is simply that you will be wise in deciding where you want to go for your doctorate to keep an open mind as to new career possibilities and areas of emphasis as you pursue your dream of getting a doctorate. There is no substitute for reading widely the descriptions of doctoral programs, internet and paper, about the universities and doctoral programs that interest you.

It is also good to know at the onset of applying for doctoral study that you will get all kinds of advice, some delivered with a good deal of conviction, as to what you should do during doctoral study in relation to future career possibilities. It is important to know that you are in the driver's seat with regard to these matters as it is *your* doctoral program, *your* career and *your* life. Our doctoral students who have realized this have a sense of self and a sense of direction that we respect and serves them well.

The following snapshot introduces us to a prospective doctoral student's trials and tribulations in deciding where to go for doctoral study. This candidate was in a sense place bound by a spouse's financial support as a teacher, having recently purchased a house in the area, and a decision to strongly consider building on contacts from a recently earned master's degree in a university near his established home.

Snapshot 2.1

Beginning the Journey to the Doctorate

I was one of those high school students who didn't take scholarship as seriously as I should have. My first two years at a small liberal arts college were much the same. It was only in my junior and senior years that I discovered how interesting and rewarding reading and writing could be.

Philosophy and history caught my attention, and I also took education classes to get the credential to teach in high school.

The education courses that really interested me were Philosophy of Education and History of Education. The professor who taught these courses had been at the college since the earth was cooling, and his dry lectures put students to sleep. I approached the professor and asked if I could help him with these two classes that interested me. He was wary at first but let me score the true-false tests he gave students as he said he was overwhelmed with work. He even let me recommend grades for students' answers to essay questions at the end of each exam with the understanding that I would not tell anyone that I was doing this.

Full of bravado, I asked the professor if I could outline a syllabus for each class, as I would like to teach these courses after going to graduate school. I had a good time doing this but only got a cursory response from the professor. Looking back on this, I realized that I had overstepped my boundaries.

Because I was a late bloomer in taking scholarship seriously, I went into a master's program in education as a full-time student immediately after receiving an undergraduate degree. I received the master's degree twelve months later. I got married nearly at the same time I graduated, and my spouse began teaching in a nearby public school.

Knowing that I wanted to get a doctorate, I visited two universities within driving distance of home. One university prided itself on its medical, dental, and law schools with the school of education relegated to a small building on the edge of the campus—a symbol of its low prestige in the university. It was obvious during my visit to the campus that my interest in history and philosophy of education was also low on the totem pole prestigious-wise in the school of education. In fact, there were few students in this program and no full-time students. I knew this was not the place for me in spite of the fact that this university was the most prestigious university in the state—what some people referred to as "the mother church."

The other university with a school of education that interested me had a land grant background and its professional schools of veterinary science, agriculture and education were given prominent places on campus. In fact, there was a beautiful new education building in the center of the campus and I must confess that this was one of the main reasons I decided to go there.

There was a strong program in history and philosophy of education in the school of education with a number of full-time students and serious part-time students as well. The curriculum was rich and varied with newly hired prominent professors from Teachers College, Columbia University and New York University on the staff along with bright and productive up-and-coming assistant professors as well.

I liked the fact that the program in history and philosophy of education had enough tradition to give me confidence in its development but was also growing in new ways that gave me the feeling that I could be a pioneer along with other doctoral students who were beginning the program. I strongly believed that programs are primarily about people—professors, administrators, students, and leaders in the field who help with internships.

The admissions people in this university liked the fact that I had a strong focus in my master's program on history and philosophy of education and wanted to extend this specialty in my doctoral program. They appreciated the way I developed my interest in history and philosophy of education in my statement of purpose. They also were impressed that my references spoke to this purpose in their letters of recommendation.

It was obvious in talking with students and professors that this was an exciting place to be. It was a school of education on the move with considerable resources to support faculty and doctoral students. Graduate assistantships for full-time students were plentiful. I applied for and received this financial support for two years.

Secretaries showed me every courtesy and gave me descriptions of courses and activities in the school of education. I was impressed by the fact that this school of education, unlike the other one I visited, had new student orientation materials. Professors invited me to attend their classes as a guest in order to see what was going on and I took them up on this offer. The doctoral student organization in the school of education also invited me to their meetings at any time. In short, it was an inviting place to be.

I therefore applied for admission and received my acceptance within a month. I had found another home.

FACTORS TO CONSIDER IN CHOOSING A PROGRAM

Geographical location of the doctoral program, given your interests, academic record and resources, has already been mentioned. Some students will travel to the other side of the country in order to have a fresh start. One aspiring doctoral student put it this way: "I did my undergraduate and master's degree at the same university in the Midwest and want to go to California to see something different. I want to teach at the university level and think that getting my doctorate in a different university in a different part of the country will make my resume stronger when I apply for a position in higher education."

Many other students decide to apply to doctoral programs near their present homes due to family responsibilities, such as the employment of a spouse or partner, children settled in a school or school system, or care for parents. We advise students who decide to go to a place for a doctorate based on geographical proximity to *not* highlight this during the application and interviewing process. In fact, a program that views you as a "sure thing" is less likely to award you fellowships and scholarships reserved for those for whom they must compete more rigorously.

One professor at the end of an applicant's interview shared the following: "We always ask students why they applied to this program at this university. When they say, 'Because of convenience' it really turns me off. It sounds like they just got off the bus and decided to get a doctorate at our university in our program, much like you reach for a box of cereal at the supermarket. They make it sound like they haven't researched the doctoral program and the professors in it."

In short, the *specific* characteristics of the doctoral program should be very important and sharing these characteristics as reasons for your application will be appreciated by those who make decisions about your admission to the program.

Quality of the Faculty and Program Administrators

Nothing is more flattering for professors and administrators in your area of doctoral interest to hear than that you want to come to their university because of the excellent faculty. This means that you need to get all of the information you can about professors who will teach you and guide you through the doctoral program. You can begin by going online to identify faculty members in the discipline or area of study in which you will get your doctorate. These listings will be under the name of the university and department that interests you.

The next step is to Google these professors so that you find out what their specific interests and kinds of expertise are. It is worth reading their most current research publications, not only so you can flatter your prospective faculty members, but also so you can determine if their research is of interest to you. Often, these are the faculty you will want to court in order to become their graduate assistants.

You will also want to know where they got their doctorates and if possible with whom they studied in their doctoral programs. For example, an aspiring doctoral student was drawn in her master's program to an area of study by a classic text. When she discovered that an assistant professor in a doctoral program that interested her was a highly regarded advisee of the author of the classic text, she was excited about the possibility of working with this up-and-coming assistant professor.

It is our experience that professors enjoy telling stories about their doctoral study in general and professors and fellow students in particular, especially those who have made it big in their chosen professions. These stories will take you backstage into the culture of doctoral programs.

You will note in listening to doctoral students that a few of their professors are known for placing their advisees who have graduated in good positions. These professors are well connected through professional and social organizations. Some simply have outgoing personalities and are likeable and generous. When these qualities are coupled with research and writing reputations that are highly respected, they are able to place their graduates with little difficulty. One of these professors was known for always paying for the first round of drinks when he was in small groups of colleagues at conventions and conferences. The following snapshot takes us backstage into his professional life.

Snapshot 2.2

Competence, Likability and the Professoriate

I grew up in a home where there was little privacy and lots of conversation. My brother, two years older, and I shared a bedroom until he went to college. My friends were always welcome in our home thanks to my mother, who always had an extra place or so at the dinner table. My coaches who were single also joined us at the dinner table quite often. My father was very gregarious and was known for his outgoing personality, something I observed each day.

I mention these things because they prepared me for a career as a professor in ways that I never thought about until I took my first position at a doctorate-granting university along with ten other assistant professors. There was an "old guard" of professors on the faculty that the administration and younger professors wanted to run off. I knew that I had to get the support of both groups in order to get tenure and an associate professorship.

At the first department faculty meeting of the year the dean asked for persons to chair various committees. Nobody wanted to be social chair, and so I volunteered for the job. I discovered that the social intelligence

I acquired in my family made me a perfect fit for the position. We had fish fries, covered dish dinners, open houses, and parties to celebrate the publication of books by faculty members as well as other achievements by colleagues.

I also had some creative ideas that became the source of lots of kidding around on the part of colleagues. For example, we collected several bikes that faculty members could ride across campus and kept them on a rack in front of our building. These bikes were called "psych bikes" because a veteran colleague who taught educational psychology donated the first bike.

I discovered from all of these activities that it doesn't cost anything to be kind to people and have fun together, and the effort it takes is repaid many times over in benefits. I moved from this university to another doctorate-granting university to get early promotion and tenure but was reminded by experiences at my first university that likability can play an important role in one's profession and life.

Lessons learned from this snapshot can be important to you as you decide where you want to go to do your doctoral study. You will probably quickly discover from your conversations with doctoral students and faculty members whether or not there is an air of good will and sociability among doctoral students, professors, and administrators. A certain amount of competitiveness is natural within the student body and among professors, but if this has crossed the line you will not feel a sense of community when you visit the campus. Leaders usually set the tone for creating and sustaining community, and you will want to give special attention to their attitudes and behavior.

You can also get information about faculty members by talking to others who know about them or have worked with them. If you had a master's program in the same or a related discipline or area of study as the doctoral program you are interested in, you can contact these professors for inside information and advice. Graduates of the doctoral program that interests you, as well as students currently in the program, can give you a good deal of information as they tell you about their experiences with professors in the program.

Graduates and present doctoral students can also give you significant input as to the role of university administrators, graduate school administrators, deans of the college or school in which you get your degree, department chairs, and doctoral program directors or coordinators. These leaders are in important decision-making positions that can affect you and your doctoral program when issues are raised and problems need to be solved. Their interpretation of rules and regulations gives them a good deal of discretionary power. Knowing something about the research and writing done by these administrators, as well as their special interests, can give you an affinity connection with them, the basis for future conversations.

Perhaps even more importantly, you need to know about people who assist these administrators for they can open or close doors for you, sometimes without your even knowing it. A doctoral student makes this point: "The assistant to the graduate school dean is known for always being on the student's side. I needed an extension of time to complete my program due to personal problems at home. The doctoral program coordinator and department chair said I would have to get the sign-off from the graduate school dean. I heard from doctoral students that Ms. Cousins, the assistant to the graduate school dean, was the person I needed to talk to face-to-face. I made an appointment to see her and she was really nice and helpful. In fact, she got the sign-off from the graduate school dean while I was there."

Conversely, you know who not to go to for help. One administrator's secretary was out-of-sorts most of the time due in large measure to the stress she was going through in caring for her aging mother who had dementia. Students learned to simply go around this secretary. On occasion, the administrator apologized for the secretary and asked people to deal directly with him.

Some of you will be attracted to a doctoral program by a professor who is recognized for his or her particular expertise. If you have a relationship with this professor before you apply to the program and you also have a strong academic record, you are virtually assured of admission to the doctoral program.

If you want to work with a professor with special expertise and don't know this person, it is wise to schedule one or more conferences to begin to develop a relationship. This will give you a sense of the chemistry you have with the professor.

In many cases, students do fine work in a master's program and are invited to become doctoral students by advisors and other professors. In fact, master's programs are a kind of training and recruiting ground for first-rate doctoral students. Continuing to work with professors you knew in your master's program has the advantage of knowing what your relationship is and where you stand with regard to your program and vocational goals. This saves you resources needed to get to know a new advocate. This is also a benefit for the professors as well.

It is simply not enough to have quality faculty. You must also find out what access you have to these faculty members. Some will be known for not being on campus much. Their external commitments, such as speaking engagements, consulting, and professional organization connections, will give you little access. Students referred to one of these professors as "the shadow" or "the ghost" because they rarely saw the real person.

Other quality faculty members truly enjoy spending time with doctoral students and will reserve blocks of time to do so. This becomes especially important at the dissertation stage. When you begin the program, however, you will spend time with your program advisor, who may or may not become your dissertation advisor at the end of the program.

Some program advisors simply sign off on paperwork and send you on your way whereas others believe that conversations with you should be an important part of your relationship and growth as a doctoral student. You should, therefore, find out how many program advisees different professors have. Current doctoral students, administrators, secretaries, and professors themselves can give you this information. You will also discover in talking to professors when you visit the campus prior to applying for the doctoral program where they stand on these issues.

While getting to know more about professors you might work with in doctoral study, you should be alert to comments about which professors have the reputation for their students completing the doctoral program. One doctoral student near the dissertation stage came up to one of us and said, "I want to have you as my dissertation advisor because other students and graduates say your students finish the program!" The word gets out rather quickly as to which advisors hang in there with their students until they graduate.

The following snapshot, in the words of a dissertation advisor, takes us backstage into the life of a professor known for having doctoral students complete their programs. It will help you identify some of the issues faculty members face in getting their advisees to the finish line.

Snapshot 2.3

The Sensitive Nature of the Dissertation Advisor's Role

Dissertation advising is one of the hardest parts of my work as a professor. I am very aware that a student's graduation involves far more than the student. Parents, other family members, friends, and colleagues have made a long term investment in something that is all-or-nothing. The doctoral student either gets the degree or not. It is a serious matter. It is not like playing horse shoes where getting close counts.

There is also a kind of closeness and intensity with the doctoral student and work at the dissertation stage that is quite different from teaching and intern advising. It is one-on-one advising, and my ego gets involved, especially if the student is doing research and writing on a subject related to my own research and writing.

During my first twenty years as a professor, I invested considerable resources in dissertation advising with at least three students receiving a doctorate each year. Students with strong research and writing skills moved along quickly and usually needed little pushing from me to complete their degrees. However, marginal students were another matter. They were able to frame the dissertation reasonably well, although they had some difficulties with research design, especially if they didn't take the dissertation seminar. They also had few problems in collecting data.

Difficulties with marginal students arose in interpreting the data and writing in a clear, well-organized and precise way. I must admit that there were times during the first twenty years of my dissertation advising when I did more than I should have in helping marginal students with their writing. All of the time, however, I received a tremendous number of strokes from students and others for going the extra mile. In fact, I gained the reputation as the professor to go to in order to be assured you would get the doctorate.

I reached the point with a few marginal students where I asked myself, "Whose doctorate is this anyway—theirs or mine?" I decided that I would cut back with these students and frequently play the role of broker identifying other people they could go to for the help they needed. I recommended excellent copyeditors and research experts they could consult. Some finished their degrees and others didn't. I felt some guilt in leaving my previous role as rescuer and probably lost some of the reputation I had established as the advisor all could go to in order to be sure they would get a doctorate.

This snapshot describes the sensitive nature of the advising role, particularly at the dissertation stage. It also illustrates the fact that you, the person searching for a doctoral program that meets your needs and desires, will not find the perfect advisor who can absolutely guarantee your getting the degree. A number of professors and administrators are needed, all of whom are human with strengths and weaknesses. Once again, don't put all of your eggs in the same basket. Build a core group of supporters to avoid being too dependent on one person.

Opportunities for changing program advisors and dissertation advisors are an important matter. Some programs will assign a program advisor to you when you begin the program. Is it possible *for you* to choose an advisor when you begin the program, based on previous relationship or knowledge you have about advisors' effectiveness? This is a matter for you to investigate if you have a program advisor in mind with whom you want to work.

You will need to ask if there is a fixed number of openings in the doctoral program and the rationale for this if it exists. Who made the decision as to the fixed number of openings? The department? The dean of the school or college? Is there any flexibility with regard to this "fixed" number? Also ask about the number of students in different phases of the doctoral program: students beginning their programs, students half-way through and students at the dissertation stage. What is the attrition rate of doctoral students? At what point do students leave the program and why? Are there provisions for continuity between coursework, comprehensive exams, and dissertation research and writing or are these phases of the program treated as discrete and separate? What are these provisions? For example, is there a dissertation seminar? Do questions on comprehensive exams simply test you once again on coursework, or do they help you transition from coursework to dissertation research and writing?

Data regarding age, gender, ethnicity, and places where students earned their undergraduate and master's degrees can be helpful. Sometimes this data is available on the programs' websites. If not, you may request this information from the program administrators. The size of classes is an issue to be explored. Are there many seminars where give and take in small groups is possible and a good deal of attention is given to research and writing in preparation for work on a dissertation? How many seminar rooms do you have? How have you accessed the electronic revolution to accommodate doctoral students?

If at all possible, you should visit the campus of the doctoral program that interests you, have discussions with doctoral students, professors, and administrators and spend time in graduate school lounges and study areas in order to listen to conversations of graduate students. This will give you a sense of the *Zeitgeist* (what's in the air) of the place.

The Quality of the Students in the Program

If you reflect on classes you had in elementary school, middle school, high school, and undergraduate school, you immediately recognize that the quality of the students in those classes was a major factor in the kind of teaching and learning that took place. Teachers had to adjust to the quality of students. Readings assigned to students and class discussions that followed were often on quite different levels even though classes or courses had the same title.

The same thing is true in doctoral level courses, seminars, and the like. Knowledge of substantive content, research and writing skills and the ability to articulate ideas in class discussions vary a good deal depending on students' backgrounds and abilities. The same thing is true with students involved in internships. Some students have rich and varied backgrounds that they bring to the internship experience and this reality influences the work they do during their internship and the discussions interns have in seminars.

It can be helpful to ask about the number of full-time students as well as the number of part-time students. What is the relationship between full-time and part-time students? Are there ways in which these students get together, or do the part-time students simply go to class and then get in their cars and go home? Are there professional organizations that serve doctoral students' needs in the doctoral program? The department? The school or college? The university?

One of the universities where we taught had several meetings sponsored by the graduate school for doctoral students during the year that focused on topics of interest to students, such as orientation to doctoral study, research and writing, and ways to successfully complete dissertation work. This was an excellent way to see likenesses and differences in the various disciplines and areas of study. It was also a vehicle for getting administrators, professors, and doctoral students together professionally and socially.

It is not unusual to have a program assemble a cohort of students who will complement one another in their program instead of looking for a single "type" of student. This model will have students progress through as a single unit, lock-step with one another in their coursework. In these cases, you will want to be especially mindful of your peers in the interview process as they will inspire or impede your success. As an aside, some students have made important contacts with peers by interviewing in multiple programs, building a base of colleagues with whom they have continued to know through the years even when they were never classmates.

When you talk to students already in the doctoral program ask them about the research and writing they have done in their classes. Ask them about the feedback professors gave them in doing this research and writing. Were their papers read by professors in a cursory way with few helpful comments, or did professors engage students in dialogue about ideas in their papers?

Ask students how they were assessed in their classes. Did professors limit their evaluation of students to so called objective tests in order to limit time needed to assess student progress? Were professors' standards high but reachable? Were professors too easy in their grading practices? Did professors refer to ways in which what students learned in classes could be helpful at the dissertation stage?

The Interview for Admission into the Doctoral Program

Many doctoral programs require applicants to be interviewed. If the department is small, all members may attend. If the department is large, an interview committee represents the larger body of professors and administrators. All participants in this process that we have known consider this mechanism for sorting students a serious matter.

As a result, it is natural for candidates for admission to be nervous. This is understood by professors and administrators involved, but students sometimes don't understand this. On one occasion a candidate was cool as a cucumber, articulate and confident in answering every question. During the discussion among professors after the candidate left the room one professor, a school psychologist, said: "You know what bothers me about this person? He didn't display a bit of nervousness. Something's wrong with him." The candidate was admitted, however.

We urge you to accept your nervousness as a natural reaction to an important challenge. Use self-talk to prepare: "I'm nervous and it is simply a way to let the persons interviewing me know that I take this seriously and care about the doctoral program." You may wish to outline some of the ideas and questions you wish to have addressed during the interview.

On another occasion, the candidate acted as if he was in his work setting rather than at the university. He welcomed the committee as they entered the room. He acted as a kind of master of ceremonies during the interview. When the candidate thought the interview should be over, he said, "I'm glad that all of you came today. Thank you for coming." The committee reminded him at this point that it was our decision as to when the interview was over. We did this in a humorous way and the candidate joined us in laughter. He was admitted to the program.

A kind of ritual takes place during the interview process. The ice is broken during the first few minutes to give the candidate a chance to get sea legs. The questions usually focus on the candidate's background, interests and reasons for applying for entrance into the doctoral program. In the hundreds of interviews we've experienced, very few candidates are aware of the research and writings of interviewers to the extent that they can talk about them in a concrete way.

On one occasion, when a student traveled across the country to attend the interview, he spoke with passion about two or three of the interviewers' writings in some detail. Those whose books and articles were honored beamed with admiration for the candidate. He was a shoe-in for admission. The prospective student was proactive and made an investment in the admissions process.

There was one candidate, a superintendent of schools, who shared the following with the doctoral admissions committee that interviewed her. "When I interview for positions as superintendent of schools I am always asked to list my accomplishments in my previous positions. Superintendents don't usually stay long in such positions and they try to jump on some band wagon or flavor of the year in order to make a name for themselves. I did that at first, but when I am interviewed now I always respond that I would like to share with them what

I learned on the job, not simply what I accomplished. And so, today I would like to share with you some of the things I would like to learn in your doctoral program." We were most impressed and she turned out to be one of the best doctoral students we ever had. She had the curiosity of the true learner.

Our advice to you as a candidate is to answer questions candidly, concisely, and precisely and then STOP. The more you say the more red flags may go up. Let the committee members talk as much as they like. Professors like to hear themselves talk! It is what we do for a living.

ISSUES YOU MAY HEAR ABOUT IN VISITING UNIVERSITIES WITH DOCTORAL PROGRAMS

A number of issues may surface as you discuss doctoral programs in universities you visit. In this section of the chapter we will share with you, the reader, a backstage view of such matters. It may well be to your advantage to know about these issues as you make final decisions about where you want to do your doctoral study, and it may also be helpful to you as you discuss problems and opportunities with others as a doctoral student.

The doctor of philosophy (Ph.D.) degree was traditionally a degree for scholars who were expected to add to research and writing in their respective disciplines or areas of study. It was referred to as a research degree. A reading knowledge of two foreign languages was required, and doctoral students were expected to take relevant courses or even establish a minor in one or more areas of study outside of their major interest of study.

With time the language requirement was reduced to one foreign language and even deleted in some Ph.D. programs with statistics and some other courses outside of their major substituted for the language requirement. Some Ph.D. programs today don't require students to take courses outside of their major area of study.

The doctor of education (Ed.D.) degree was introduced as an alternative to the Ph.D. program. It was largely designed for practitioners. There is no language requirement, and classes outside the discipline or area of study are frequently not required. Ed.D. students are expected to be primarily consumers of research rather than producers of research.

As noted earlier, a number of cohort programs have been introduced so that a group of students are with each other from start to finish of the Ed.D. degree. This has the advantage of getting to know these students well and the disadvantage of not getting to know more students.

Distance education doctoral programs were started with professors traveling to sites near students' homes and work places. With time, many of these Ed.D.

programs offered more and more online courses with some programs having all courses online. The University of Phoenix is the best known example of the latter. You may go online with any search engine under Online Doctoral Programs to fine a large number of non-traditional programs that are strictly online. An obvious advantage for students in online doctoral programs is that they can keep full-time jobs and go online to fit into their work schedules.

Universities are able to experience great financial savings by not having to pay travel expenses and the like for professors. Classrooms do not have to be provided, another cost cutter. The technological advances have allowed for these changes to occur and for programs to find creative means to effectively train students.

Some Ed.D. programs that initially established the credibility of their programs by flying in nationally known professors to off-campus sites no longer needed such professors. The national reputations of online instructors were of lesser consequence. This reduced the amount of money needed for instruction, offset in part by the institutional costs of technology and related supports. Online instruction also had the advantage of eliminating bad-weather problems for professors and students. No face-to-face contact with students also minimized other problems, such as sexual harassment lawsuits.

Ed.D. programs grew a good deal as school boards and other hiring agencies expected superintendents of schools to have doctorates. Therefore, principals and central office leaders who wanted to be considered for superintendent of schools positions entered Ed.D. programs.

It is important that you know that there is an effort led by the Carnegie Foundation for the Advancement of Teaching, in Stanford, California to use a national network of nearly two dozen colleges and universities to recraft and gear the Ed.D. more for practitioners rather than for professional scholars (Archer, 2007). Lee S. Shulman, a renowned scholar and the foundation's president, led this effort.

Participants in this movement believe that the quality of work in the Ed.D. program will be lifted, rather than lowered, by a curriculum focused on preparing candidates for the highest levels of leadership in educational practice. It is argued that coursework should reflect job-related issues, and the final projects should be more practitioner oriented in contrast to dissertations in a Ph.D. program.

The recrafted Ed.D. for practitioners is not designed to prepare graduates for work in academia. Some universities will retain their Ph.D. programs in education in order to prepare scholars and researchers for positions in academia while at the same time building the new Ed.D. program.

In the case of the counseling field, most programs who previously offered the Ed.D. now offer the Ph.D. for those who plan to enter the professorate. Even those in clinical settings perceive the Ph.D. to be better recognized than the Ed.D. as it appears more comparable to their psychology counterpart's Ph.D. This has caused many programs to drop the Ed.D. entirely as they are less able to compete with those who have transitioned.

One thing you should keep an eye out for in considering doctoral study is whether or not there is conflict in parts of the school of education, such as the educational leadership department and the curriculum department, between scholars and practitioners. The question you will need to address, if such a conflict exists, is "What are the implications of this for me, given my professional goals?" It will not take you long to determine whether or not there is a well-functioning mix of scholars and practitioners in the department where the doctoral program you are interested in is housed.

Some institutions and schools of education deliberately blur the distinction between the Ph.D. and Ed.D. The issue is too sensitive, a can of worms that raises questions about the quality of doctoral degrees held by members of the faculty. When the issue is raised, professors end up defending the quality of scholarship they experienced where they earned their doctorates.

We have been on search committees where doctoral graduates from some institutions of higher education have not survived the first cut for tenure track positions simply because of the poor reputation of the doctoral program where they got their degree. Doctoral graduates from such institutions of higher education are shocked and angry when they hear informally that they are eliminated from consideration for desired positions simply because of the reputation of the program from which they graduated. They were not apprised of this by program leaders when they entered the doctoral program from which they earned their degree.

If you are interested in pursuing a career as a professor or administrator in higher education, you will need to talk with people in positions like the one that interests you in order to get the straight scoop on these matters. It is important to remember that all persons with doctorates are sensitive to criticism about the kind of doctorate they have, the discipline in which the doctorate is located, and the university where they earned the doctorate. The more you get into issues like the one in this section of the chapter, the more you will realize that all human institutions, including the professoriate are full of contradictions. (See appendix E, "Dealing with Contradictions in a Doctoral Program.")

A second issue that you may hear discussed as you consider where you wish to get your doctorate is the relationship, if any, that professors in the doctoral program see between teaching, research, and writing. The publish or perish mantra assumes that there is little if any connection between teaching and research and writing. And yet, there are professors who see their teaching, especially in doctoral level seminars, as a place to try out new ideas that make their way into their writing. It is this promising view of the professoriate that can benefit you as a doctoral student, especially if you are interested in pursuing a career as a professor. These professors will instruct you through their example as to how to integrate teaching, research and writing.

We hope that our brief introduction to this issue will help you find an advisor and committee members who will be like-minded with you in the interest of working toward a definition of work and occupation that will be meaningful in your life.

Possible Scholarship and Fellowship Opportunities

You may wish to turn to chapter 4, *Graduate Assistantships, Internships and Fellowships,* for a description of these sources of support for doctoral students. You should be alert before applying to doctoral programs to those programs that depend on teaching assistantships as a kind of "cash cow" that give professors released time at the expense of doctoral students. If you are overinvolved with teaching, it will be at the expense of your own research, writing and attention to coursework requirements. Some of our doctoral students, naturally needing financial support, take on an extra section or two of teaching. They are then stretched to complete other parts of their doctoral program and lives.

It is surprising how many scholarships are overlooked by students who qualify for them. For example, a Native American doctoral student realized late in her program that she qualified for a scholarship earmarked for Native American doctoral students. She received the scholarship for one year whereas if she had known of it earlier, she could have had it for two previous years of full-time study. Instead she had worked part-time off-campus to support herself. The graduate school was delighted that the scholarship was finally used by someone.

Fellowships are usually prestigious when given by a university on the basis of merit and previous academic record. Portable fellowships are granted by the federal government and private agencies and are not usually based on merit alone. Need and other factors are also considered.

There are scholarship and fellowship offices on most campuses that will give you information that can be valuable. Being proactive is once again very important.

The Point of all of This

All of the comments and questions in this chapter are designed to help you see if there is a good fit between your aspirations, professional and personal, and the doctoral program's offerings. There is also a bonus in giving attention to the issues discussed in this chapter. You will demonstrate to professors and administrators, especially those involved in deciding who gets into the doctoral program, that you have done your homework.

Stage II

How to Thrive in your
Doctoral Program

You have now prepared the way for beginning your doctoral program by assessing where you are in your life and career, applying for one or more doctoral programs, receiving word as to where you are accepted, and making a decision to enter a particular program. One of the first things you will notice now that you are a beginning doctoral student is how your perspective on the doctoral program differs from what you experienced as a master's student. Your master's program primarily focused on coursework. Once you completed your coursework, you received your degree.

Some of you wrote a master's thesis, and yet you are now aware that the dissertation, like the doctoral program itself, is broader in scope, more time consuming, and more demanding in other ways as well. In short, your investment of resources in the doctoral program will be much greater than you experienced in the master's program.

Chapter 3, "Composing Inner Curriculum and Influencing Outer Curriculum in Doctoral Study," gives attention to the doctoral course of study created by professors and administrators in the university, the graduate school, the college and/or school and the department in which the degree is lodged (what we call the outer curriculum) and what you learn during the time you are a doctoral student (what we call the inner curriculum.)

Your participation in the doctoral program, as well as that of your fellow students, will influence the formal course of study in this process. For example, your successes and difficulties in the doctoral program will be observed by professors and administrators thus influencing, keeping some things and changing others, the doctoral course of study in place for students who follow you after your graduation. Examples of this have been noted by former Yale Professor of Psychology Seymour B. Sarason. (See appendix J,

"A Conversation with Seymour B. Sarason About the Creation and Dynamics of the Dissertation Committee.")

We conclude chapter 3 with a discussion of the importance of having a strategy for information gathering and reflection as you make your way along the doctoral program path toward graduation, a system that will be especially valuable at the dissertation stage. Specific ways to implement this strategy are spelled out.

In chapter 4, "Obtaining and Maintaining Graduate Assistantships and Internships," we discuss some of the opportunities you will have to acquire skills that may stand you well after you receive your doctorate. What you learn from one or more of these positions will also complement what you experienced during your coursework. Your leadership will be strengthened, and your resume will demonstrate to those interested in hiring you for positions in higher education that you can do what they will want you to do in colleges and universities.

Chapter 5, "Comprehensive Examinations," will describe some of those things you will be expected to know in written and oral presentations assessed by your professors. Clear, coherent, precise, and concise writing as well as oral presentation of self skills are noted in this chapter. We will discuss back-stage matters and suggest tips to ensure your success.

"Researching and Writing the Dissertation," the title of chapter 6, is obviously a matter than invokes a good deal of anxiety in doctoral students. You have probably already been introduced to the ominous All-But-the-Dissertation (ABD) phenomenon. We take you in some detail through the various stages of dissertation research and writing in this chapter: Sources of Guidance, Reviewing the Literature, Choosing Research Topics, Developing a Proposal, Research Design, Interpreting the Results, Writing the Finished Product and Oral Defense. We give particular attention to ways to avoid pitfalls in doing dissertation research and writing.

Chapter 3

Composing Inner Curriculum and Influencing Outer Curriculum in Doctoral Study

Reflection is nothing less than internal dialogue with oneself. It is the process of bringing past experiences to a conscious level, analyzing them, and determining better ways to think and behave in the future.

—Frank McCourt (2005, pp. xxi–xxii)

We have a deep tendency to see the changes we need to make as being in our outer world, not in our inner world. It is challenging to think that while we redesign the manifest structures of our organizations, we must also redesign the internal structures of our "mental models."

—Peter Senge (1990, p. xv)

Self-authority is the single most important radical idea there is, and there is a real hunger for putting the personal and the external back together again.

—Gloria Steinem (1992, p. 55)

The greatest trap in life is not success, popularity, or power, but self-rejection, doubting who we truly are.

—Henri Nouwen (2006, p. 30)

One of the first questions you may ask as a beginning doctoral student is "What courses will I take in the doctoral program?" The question is understandable, given the fact that you have had more than twenty years of formal education during which you have been expected to cover bodies of knowledge *introduced by teachers and professors* in a curriculum, traditionally defined as a course of study. We refer to this as the "outer curriculum," as it predates your reacting to and learning from it. We speak of *influencing* the outer curriculum as the locus of control is in the hands of others rather than you, the doctoral student.

"Inner curriculum" is what happens within you, the learner, as you create meaning from exposure to what is going on outside of you, including the "outer curriculum" or course of study (Brubaker, 2004, pp. 20–24). We therefore refer to *composing* the inner curriculum as the locus of control is with you, the doctoral student. To compose is to create, not simply influence.

In the remainder of this chapter we will describe ways in which you, the doctoral student, will be afforded more opportunities to influence the creation of the doctoral program's outer curriculum as you move through the program. You will feel increased ownership in the outer curriculum of the program as well as more responsibility for the program's success.

This is especially true at the dissertation stage as there is a shift from an external focus of control to an internal one. When you defend your dissertation in front of your committee, you will be considered an "expert" with regard to your research and writing. As a result of your increased ownership and participation, the outer curriculum will become a richer springboard for your inner curriculum's growth and development. You will have nurtured your own professional development and your fellow students and professors may well have done likewise as a result of your active involvement in the doctoral program.

You and your fellow students will leave behind a legacy of scholarship that will be a part of the culture of the doctoral program, the department, the school or college, and the university itself. In fact, the credibility of these units of the university rests on the quality of work you, fellow doctoral students, professors, and administrators do. This is a matter of considerable influence indeed! When you walk across the stage to receive your doctorate, you will have a sense of pride in your program, your university, and yourself.

As a beginning doctoral student, you have had years of experience in becoming a successful professional student who locates authority in the outer curriculum and those who deliver it—teachers, professors, textbook authors, and others. The following snapshot describes what happened when I, Dale Brubaker, challenged this system as a senior in college.

Snapshot 3.1

A Lesson Learned the Hard Way

It was my last semester as an undergraduate in a liberal arts college. It was time to take my final exam in the World Religions class. During the semester I took classes in world drama, world literature, and world history. While sitting behind my desk in a rented room, I sifted through my notes from my four classes and started connecting insights. Major concepts served as organizing devices as I began to pull things together like working on a puzzle on a rainy day. I sensed that I was creating a framework of knowledge *that I had created.*

I entered the World Religions classroom the next morning with a quiet confidence. I seemed to lose track of time as I integrated learning from my four classes in order to write answers to the essay questions. I sensed that I was writing intellectual history, as my history professor defined it, seeing the whole picture rather than bits and pieces of the picture. It was such a satisfying feeling. What I didn't realize was that I was in the eye of a perfect storm by questioning the World Religions' professor's way of organizing knowledge for his instructional purposes.

The next morning I received a phone call from the professor asking me to come to his office as soon as possible to discuss my answers to the exam. He was friendly but troubled by what I had written. He said, "I only wanted you to write about what you had learned in my class." I left his office with an exam grade of C+, what he believed was an acceptable compromise between his expectations and my creative writing. My first thought was one of keen disappointment and rejection. I said to myself, "I didn't play the game and I paid the price!"

Although most doctoral programs do not lock step students through a series of required courses, you may still find it an adjustment to move from the reactor role to the actor role in doctoral study. Some of the courses you take in doctoral study will have a more traditional format with highly prescribed steps to follow in order to successfully meet professors' expectations. You will have the security of knowing exactly what is expected of you and when you are expected to meet these assignments. Other courses will afford you opportunities to work more independently and create your own structures that will invite reactions from your professors.

There are also professors who will invite you to experience important learning outside of classrooms and coursework. The following snapshot illustrates what happened when a doctoral student accepted this invitation.

Snapshot 3.2

Being Welcomed to a Backstage View of the Professoriate

I was surprised at the beginning of my doctoral program when Professor James Macdonald at the University of Wisconsin, Milwaukee, took me "under his wing" and included me in a number of informal activities that helped me understand what it is like to be a professor. As I look back on this, I realize that this was the beginning of his role as my mentor.

He invited me to have lunch at a German restaurant with him and a colleague during which they discussed starting a new program in humanistic education. I reminded myself that my role was largely that of a listener unless they asked for my opinion during the conversation. The discussion started slowly but became more animated when they talked about ways in which public schools and the university could work together to create curriculum materials that would integrate thinking, feeling, and acting.

At this point, Dr. Macdonald reached for a napkin, took a pen out of his shirt pocket and began sketching a framework for the curriculum materials. I glanced at it and discovered ENDS (objectives) at the top of the napkin followed below by MEANS (methods, materials, and evaluation).

Professor Macdonald's colleague looked at the napkin, became agitated and said, "Jim, you have just used the Tyler Rationale, the very framework that you have spent much of your career criticizing. [Ralph Tyler, a professor at Stanford University, wrote a book, *Basic Principles of Curriculum and Instruction* (1949), that became the basis for most lesson plans: select objectives and put them in behavioral terms, select and organize activities (methods and materials) for student learning; and evaluate their effectiveness in reaching objectives.]

Dr. Macdonald looked at his colleague and softly replied, "We have to start somewhere." His colleague responded: "You sound like one of my professors in doctoral study, George S. Counts. He said that he wanted his children raised as Methodists so that they would have something to reject."

The conversation continued for another hour, during which a name was given to the program, The University of Wisconsin-Milwaukee Humanistic Education Project. It was decided that professors would be invited to write occasional papers that would be published, and a book would be written in order to distribute curriculum materials being developed.

But the main thing I remember from this lunch together is that I got a backstage view and feeling about what it is like to be a professor. In a sense, I felt welcomed into "the club" as a professor by being a part of this backstage conversation between two professors. I experienced the power of relationships for professors and doctoral students.

I considered this one of the first opportunities to develop my research base, something that could be especially helpful to me at the dissertation stage of the program. I sensed that doctoral study could have a richness to it that I had not experienced in my formal education before and I wanted to take every opportunity I could to experience things like this.

STRATEGIES FOR COMPOSING YOUR INNER CURRICULUM AND INFLUENCING THE OUTER CURRICULUM

Now that you have been introduced to the distinction between outer curriculum and inner curriculum, it should be clear that you can play a significant part in moving from the reactor role to the actor role, thus enriching your inner curriculum. This is especially important as you move toward the most independent phase of the doctoral program, dissertation research and writing.

The question before you is, "What experiences, gifts, and talents from my past can I capitalize on and build on in my doctoral study?" It follows that the more confidence you gain the more your dignity as a person and doctoral student will be affirmed. We have identified four key strategies for developing your inner curriculum and influencing the outer curriculum, each of which will be discussed in the following sections.

Strategy 1: Understand that you don't enter the doctoral program as an empty vessel or blank sheet of paper.

It is easy for you and your professors to fall into a deficit model whereby it is assumed that you know nothing or nothing of value when you begin doctoral study. The way to challenge this assumption is to recognize and celebrate the talents and learning experiences you have accumulated before entering the doctoral program.

One way to be engaged in this process is by doing professional autobiography with a special eye out for coherence in the body of work you experienced prior to doctoral study. In other words, "How did you use your talents to do things that fit together in some kind of meaningful framework that we choose to call a body of work?"

What is work? It is the exertion of effort to accomplish things that you think are important. You assess the sources of power available to you and then draw upon them to capitalize on opportunities available to you. It is in doing this that you will experience what Malcolm Gladwell (2008) calls "the miracle of meaningful work" (p. 269). Four sources of power available to you as you engage in this work are positional authority, charisma, succor, and expertise (Brubaker, 2004, pp. 89–91).

Positional authority is power by virtue of your position in an organization or setting. We commonly associate it with bureaucratic forms of organization, for those with more positional authority give commands to those subordinates who have less. Regardless of the respect, or lack of it, accorded the person with positional authority, the bureaucratic subordinate is expected to obey such commands.

You may have used positional authority in jobs you held prior to doctoral study. As a doctoral student you may become a teaching assistant or program administrator during an internship that will afford you positional authority.

Charisma is a kind of magnetic charm that draws upon nonverbal messages, such as smiles and nods of approval, as well as speaking. We think of persons who use charisma as energetic and inspirational. Styles of dress and a leader's bearing are often cited when we refer to charismatic leaders. For better or worse, it is also associated with attractiveness on some occasions.

You probably have honed the use of charisma in formal and informal settings when you were a student before entering the doctoral program, and you will also use charisma as you move through the doctoral program. If so, you will be considered an appealing person to be around, and you will use this source of power in formal and informal settings as you communicate with others. A sense of humor is often part of charismatic presentation of self.

Succor is an informal kind of power that leaves others with the feeling that they are supported emotionally. It is commonly associated with counseling and coaching. "You can do it" is the message conveyed. It is an important source of power in team building. You have been a valued small group member and friend in drawing on succor as a source of power prior to doctoral study and will continue to encourage, counsel, and coach others in doctoral study. You will celebrate others' victories and pick them up when they are down. (See appendix F, "Working Alone and Working as a Team Member.)

Expertise is a source of power attributed to persons because of their recognized ability to do something well. Respect is often the word that is used in association with an expert in an organization or setting. You may have special skills in handling details and writing reports that stood you well before beginning doctoral study and will also be valued as you work toward completion of your doctorate.

The same may be true of your communication skills. Some kinds of expertise, such as public speaking, are highly visible whereas other kinds are less obvious. (See appendix I, "How Good and Comfortable Are You as a Speaker and Listener.)

It is a combination of these sources of power used within a particular context that will help you continue to bring excellence to your body of work. The satisfaction that this will bring to you and others in doing doctoral student work is of immeasurable value.

The following snapshot will demonstrate how one doctoral student shared a professional autobiography that integrated sources of power in order to bring coherence to a body of work. (See appendix A, "Bringing Coherence to the Body of Work You've Done in Preparation for Doctoral Study.")

Snapshot 3.3

Finding Meaning in Doing My Professional Autobiography

I was surprised when the professor in my first course in doctoral study, an orientation to the program itself, asked us to begin thinking about our professional autobiographies. She took us back to some of the lessons she had learned in life prior to her starting her doctoral program a decade or so ago.

She also talked about how these lessons were helpful to her in successfully completing her doctoral program. For example, she said that she had been editor of the newspaper in high school, and this experience taught her to reconcile differences between persons with opposing points of view.

She added that her experience on a debate team in college taught her to articulate and defend a point of view she supported. She candidly admitted this experience taught her that on occasion a person needs a kind of guile or slyness in presenting one's best self to others. The smile on her face while saying this told us that she knew how to take care of herself.

It was at this point in our professor's presentation that I began to see how many of my experiences in the world of work could be valuable in my doctoral program. I had learned to play the game of student in K-12 education and higher education well enough to get good grades and the approval of my teachers and professors.

I also had a variety of jobs from middle school through college that taught me what I would call "people skills." I cleaned the waiting room and bathrooms in an optometrist's office, served as a surveyor's assistant, worked on the line in a college cafeteria, scrubbed pots and pans in a girl's dorm, did custodial work in the same dorm, and was an advisor in a men's residence hall. Getting and keeping these jobs taught me to work with all kinds of people and I felt like an important member of a team each step of the way.

My position as a teacher in a high school for three years gave me the confidence to stand up in front of more than a hundred people a day. At first I simply survived, during the second year I creatively survived, and the third year I became a professional. I not only learned to manage a classroom but I also discovered many different ways to involve students in the learning process.

I hope to be a teaching assistant during my doctoral program and believe my high school teaching experience will give me the confidence to do well in this role. I may well seek a professorship after receiving my doctorate.

I had the opportunity as an English major in college to build on my position as editor of the high school yearbook. This background prompted me to write a senior paper in college and in the process I was introduced to several qualitative research methodologies—narrative research and case study research in particular. I want to expand on these qualitative research methodologies in my doctoral program, and I also want to explore ways in which quantitative research can be blended with qualitative research methodologies. I'm somewhat anxious about this but believe I can handle it.

What we see emerging from this snapshot is how the beginning doctoral student is starting to discoverer coherence in the body of work she experienced prior to doctoral study. The doctoral student is also starting to see connections with what she anticipates in the doctoral program she has just entered. The meaning the student has already discovered in this process should be very inspirational in moving forward in the doctoral program. Analytical intelligence will be enriched by practical intelligence as a result of new understandings and activities.

It is also interesting to note that the doctoral student in the snapshot has used all four sources of power in order to come to an understanding of personal talents and opportunities. Opportunities for learning and advancement were capitalized on at each stage of the student's life—from high school student to college student to high school teacher to doctoral student.

The doctoral student's story demonstrates the power of creating a strong support system that merges outer and inner curriculums. Each influences the other in a dynamic way so that some things are conserved whereas other things are changed.

Strategy 2: Assess the talents and interests of professors and others who are involved in working with doctoral students.

Some of these people will play a formal role in your program. They may be members or even the chair of your program committee and/or your dissertation committee. They and others may be professors of the classes you take. But, it is important to remind yourself that there are many persons in the university who may be extremely valuable to you in a more informal role.

They may be joined by people in the community, the nation, and the world in giving you precisely the kind of help you need at a particular time during doctoral study. It only remains for you to play a proactive role in seeking them out and establishing the kinds of relationship you need to achieve your purposes. Modern communication systems make all of this possible.

You will probably be assigned a temporary or provisional program advisor to get you started in doctoral study unless you have a previous connection with a person you want to play this role. It is important for you to know if there are provisions for changing this temporary advisor to a permanent advisor of your choice prior to filing your program of study with the department, academic school, or college in which the department is located and the graduate school.

Note that this program of study, when signed off by designated persons, is your contract with the university. This is especially important to remember if there are changes in your committee membership due to faculty retirements, moves by one or more committee members to other universities, and the like. Once again, the program of study with regard to courses to be taken, may remain the same even though other things, like comprehensive exam questions, or will be different due to a new person or persons on the committee.

Some provisional program advisors define their role as primarily an administrative one. They will help you with the details needing attention and the forms that need to be acquired and signed. If the advisor defines his role as primarily an administrative one, you should use your communication network to find out if the advisor has a reputation for being on top of details and can be counted on to help you in a timely manner. (See appendix D, "The 'Table Manners' of Doctoral Student Leadership.")

Other provisional program advisors play more of a mentoring role and give attention to course content, career goals and opportunities for cooperative research and writings. In short, they pay attention to you in a more personal way. You will want to check the reputation of the program committee advisor for dealing with administrative details. In the event that this reputation is tarnished, you will need to handle these details yourself and in effect guide the advisor with regard to the management of details.

The choice of who should be members of your program advisory committee is a decision that should be mutually acceptable to you and your program advisor. It is to your advantage if your advisor has the respect of committee members, tenure, and at least an associate professorship. This increases the chances of junior faculty members on the committee supporting the chair's recommendations and also makes it more likely that the chair will not move to another university in the near future.

It is important to note that the program planning committee has its own personality that must be considered by you and your program chair. Students often make the mistake of thinking that their one-on-one relationships with individual faculty members will ensure a fine working committee.

Conflicting personalities and ideologies must be avoided if at all possible. Your temporary advisor's ability to prevent and/or deal constructively with such conflict is crucial. Interpersonal histories of faculty members may be important, but harder to determine. Your being discrete about backstage information your program advisor gives you concerning possible committee members is absolutely essential.

Provisional advisors have different leadership styles. It is important that you find out what these styles are, often by talking to doctoral graduates as well as students still in the doctoral program. One thing to look for is an advisor who has students who are moving along well toward graduation. Conversely, you may recognize professors with many all-but-dissertation (ABD) doctoral students who have made little progress towards completion over an extended period of time.

One note for those wishing to complete the program: CAUTION. Advisors who are unpredictable can also be a problem They can be affable and nice but unreliable. Some advisors are perfectionists who repeatedly change their minds and expectations in the interest of perfecting your work. The result is that you will be slowed down time and time again and feel off balance in working toward the completion of your degree.

The distinction between doctoral student needs and desires can be helpful. The wise and competent advisor will sometimes bring to your attention the fact that something you desire isn't what you need. A simple example is the distinction between the student's desire to do dissertation work that will save the world, only to be reminded by an advisor that he or she needs four or five sign-offs to complete the degree.

Younger faculty members, who have recently joined the faculty, can play an important role as committee members. This is particularly true if there is something in it for them. For example, they are up on the most recent research and writing in their field of interest and may wish to share this knowledge with you and other doctoral students. They may wish to have you consider extending their research and writing and even co-authoring articles with you.

The key question that should guide you in dealing with all of these matters is *"Who will help me complete this doctoral program in the most efficient and effective way?"*

Doctoral students sometimes move beyond professional relationships with professors in general and committee chairs and committee members in particular to form personal or social relationships. The following snapshot offers us an example of this.

Snapshot 3.4

The Upside and Downside of Socializing with Professors

I am a gregarious person by nature and have socialized with persons in all stations of life from the time I was a child in a small town. I probably learned this from my father, who was a minister raised in a large family.

It seemed natural for me in doctoral study to get together with students and professors who shared similar interests. One of my philosophy professors, who introduced me to linguistic analysis and its role in ethics, was a tennis player. George Kerner and I played tennis once a week during the good weather season over a three year period, and my wife and I invited him over for dinner several times, something he especially appreciated as a single man. I was a good student, and we seemed to have the kind of relationship that was enjoyed by both of us with no apparent problems.

An intellectual historian and I became handball partners during the winter months. He introduced me to visiting historians, and I had dinner with them and saw their personal sides in a way that I would not have otherwise experienced. One of the visiting historians, D W. Brogan, helped me with an independent study that made a major contribution to my dissertation. The independent study helped me explore the concept of national character.

My relationship with the intellectual historian was difficult at times as he was an alcoholic. I was young and didn't understand the implications of alcoholism at the time. Problems with him were complicated by the fact that he was a member of my four-person doctoral committee. I consistently received A grades on my seminar papers and final course evaluations. One semester I was assigned a B in his class. When I asked him about this he replied, "You beat me too often in handball."

I simply went on with my life and didn't complain. He failed to show up at my dissertation defense although he told me earlier that he liked my research and writing. The doctoral committee, upon hearing of this, told me to get his signature on the necessary paper work. I got his signature after finding him at the Merry-Go-Round Bar and sitting with him for an hour or so. I drank Cokes to stay absolutely sober, whereas he had something stronger.

Needless to say, I discovered from this experience what the upside and downside of social relationships with professors can be, particularly those on a doctoral committee. An upside was that I stayed motivated and connected to the doctoral program. On the downside, social relationships can be energy draining, and one can lose the original focus of moving efficiently and effectively toward completion of the program. Those on the downside should be avoided if possible and dealt with the best one can if encountered.

Relationships between professors and doctoral students of a more intimate nature are part of the folklore of the professoriate. Novels, often written by English professors, and movies pick up on the various themes associated with such relationships and are humorous if observed from a safe distance. How can the problematic behavior of professors and doctoral students be explained? Rather simply stated, the personal needs and desires of some professors and their doctoral students blind them to the difficulties created by parties to such relationships.

What advice is best for you to follow? Avoid such relationships personally and remember that when you talk about others in such relationships each person you talk to will probably tell at least one other person. Your comments may come back to bite you.

Strategy 3: Maintain a positive attitude while being realistic about the pitfalls that may slow your momentum.

Finding ways to keep a positive attitude in doctoral study will help you avoid the kind of self-rejection Henri Rouwen cites in a header quote that introduces this chapter. Momentum is essential in as sizable a goal as completing a doctoral degree, and challenges, both external and internal, will be aplenty. As you coach yourself through this process, it will be important to have a refined understanding of a positive attitude. A doctoral student speaks to this challenge in the following snapshot.

Snapshot 3.5

When Difficult Things Happen to Challenge a Doctoral Student's Optimism

I was raised in a family where we were expected to be positive and optimistic. "Who wants to spend time around a grouchy person!" my father said repeatedly.

He was rewarded in his profession by many people who found him a relief from the negativism in other parts of their lives. His optimism was often revealed in poetry that he recited when he suspected we were not optimistic: "From the day you are born 'til you ride in a hearse, there's nothing that happened that couldn't have been worse." Occasionally someone would say that I was in denial for being so optimistic, but most people said they liked my positive attitude toward life.

I was introduced to M. Scott Peck's writings in one of my graduate classes and the professor said that Peck's worldview would challenge some of us to confront our own worldviews. The professor argued that our "inner curriculum," our basic assumptions about reality, were central to the kind of leadership we would display in doctoral studies and beyond. He warned us to "tighten our seatbelts" as we read and discussed Peck's writing in one of the assigned texts, *The Road Less Traveled* (1978).

The first sentence of the first chapter, "Problems and Pain," is "Life is difficult" (p. 15). He continues, "What makes life difficult is that the process of confronting and solving problems is a painful one. Yet it is in this whole process of meeting and solving problems that life has its meaning" (p. 15).

It struck me that this is another definition of learning, and not to recognize the role of suffering in these matters causes us to pay a greater price. Peck quotes noted psychologist Carl Jung to describe this price: "Neurosis is always a substitute for legitimate suffering" (Jung, C. 1973, p. 75).

Peck (1978) continues to develop his thesis: "Discipline is the basic set of tools we require to solve life's problems" (p. 15). He adds: "What are these tools, these techniques of suffering, these means of experiencing the pain of problems constructively that I call discipline? There are four: delaying of gratification, acceptance of responsibility, dedication to truth, and balancing. The problem lies not in the complexity of these tools but in the will to use them" (p. 18).

It became clear to me that Peck's worldview challenged the extreme view of optimism passed on to me by my father. In adopting this worldview, I was in the state of denial in dealing with some of life's problem. I stated this with some hesitancy in my small graduate class and the professor had an interesting response: "Martin Luther King, Jr. spoke to this matter in a speech at Central Methodist Church in Detroit, less than a month before his death on April 4, 1968.

"He made a distinction between hope and optimism, criticizing some optimists who believed that things would naturally work out just fine without investing any resources in solving problems. He referred to this

as 'magic hope,' a verbal slight of hand that would excuse such optimists from doing the hard work necessary in the civil rights movement"
(Brubaker & Coble, 2005, p. 104).

I spent some time taking in all of these ideas and committed myself to
being hopeful in facing difficulties in life in general and the doctoral program in particular without falling into the trap of extreme optimism and
the denial of the hard work necessary to work through very real problems.
I've found this hard psychological work at times but extremely gratifying
when I see the light at the end of the tunnel.

An example of this is that I realized I could learn something from all
professors even when their annoying idiosyncrasies kept me from asking
me to be on my program and dissertation committees. I didn't need to be
in their classes to learn from them by listening to their speeches and reading their writings. I interviewed one professor who was an expert in the
research methodology I wanted to use in my dissertation and got useful
information even though I never took a class from him. I learned not to
think in all-or-nothing terms. This learning gave me better quality of life
as a doctoral student and leader.

There is a tremendous amount of time, energy, talent, and other resources
involved in getting a doctorate. It follows that there are at times distortions in
thinking that must be faced head-on and honestly. Avoiding and/or dealing
with these cognitive distortions is an essential part of maintaining a positive
attitude in doctoral study.

A professor who taught an orientation seminar required of all doctoral
students was aware of Strategy 3's emphasis on maintaining a positive attitude and avoiding pitfalls that would slow down students in their quest for
the doctorate. The professor was convinced after working with hundreds
of students that distortions in their thinking and behavior needed to be
addressed head-on in the seminar. His mechanism for dealing with this issue
was a framework created by David Burns, author of *Feeling Good: The New
Mood Therapy* (2009). The framework consisted of ten cognitive distortions
as follows:

1. *All-or-nothing thinking* refers to the "tendency to evaluate your personal
   qualities in extreme, black-or-white categories" (Burns, 1980, p. 31).
   I was a straight-A student in my master's program and expected to do
   likewise in doctoral study. When I received a B in a Formal Logic class,
   my first thought was "I just know that I don't have what it takes." When
   sharing this view with a couple of my friends in the class, I realized that

the professor only gave one A and it was to his advisee in the Philosophy Department. The reality of this situation brought me back to earth.

2. *Overgeneralization* is to "arbitrarily conclude that one thing that happened to you once will occur over and over again" (Burns, 1980, p. 32). When I began teaching a master's level course as part of my graduate assistant-ship, I had a problem during the first few weeks. I would ask a question and almost no students responded. I was excited about the materials I was presenting but students didn't seem to share this enthusiasm. I mistakenly concluded that graduate-school teaching was not for me. Interestingly enough, however, once the students warmed up to my teaching they became more involved, and my anxiety abated.

3. A *mental filter* is in place when "you pick out a negative detail in any situation and dwell on it exclusively, thus perceiving that the whole situation is negative" (Burns, 1980, p. 33). I am primarily a left-brained person who loves linear-sequential thinking and details. I had a right-brained professor who wandered here and there without following the syllabus each week.

   I became so obsessed with this fact that it kept me from understanding and appreciating what the professor was trying to do. About half way through the course, I realized that the professor's approach was useful in generating ideas for dissertation research and writing. In fact, I discovered one of these ideas that became the basis for my dissertation work.

4. *Disqualifying the positive* takes place when "you don't just ignore positive experiences, you cleverly and swiftly turn them into their nightmarish opposite" (Burns, 1980, p. 34). Two other doctoral students invited me to lunch. After the lunch, one of the students asked me why I was so critical of some of the people we discussed at the luncheon. I didn't like to hear this but I responded: "I guess it's because of the anxiety I feel about my own ability as a doctoral student." I learned a lesson the hard way but it is one I needed to give attention to and try to correct.

5. *Jumping to conclusions* takes place when "you automatically jump to a conclusion that is not justified by the facts of the situation" (Burns, 1980, p. 35). This is a kind of *mind reading* because "you make the assumption that other people are looking down on you and you're so convinced about this that you don't even bother to check it out" (Burns, 1980, p. 35).

   I don't know why, but I had the habit of discounting positive things students said about me and my scholarship. One student called me on this: "Why do you always react this way when I compliment you on your work?" My response surprised even me: "I just wanted to beat you to the punch in criticizing me."

   My response seemed stupid to me as well as my friend and we laughed about it. I learned from this that accepting compliments is a gracious thing to do, and I needed to practice doing this until it became part of who I am. With time, this was a gift I gave to myself.

6. *Magnification and minimization* occur when "you are either blowing things up out of proportion or shrinking them" (Burns, 1980, p. 36). "If I send this e-mail to my advisor trying to change the date of the meeting, she'll think I'm fickle" is an example of magnification. "My advisor won't even notice this e-mail" is an example of minimization.

7. *Emotional reasoning* exists when "you take your emotions as evidence of the truth" (Burns, 1980, p. 37). "I don't ever want to give speeches in formal settings" serves as an example. I felt this way until my advisor suggested that I try to use some of my informal communication skills, such as moving out from behind the lectern and using an outline rather than reading my speech. I tried doing this and it really worked.

8. *Should statements* are an attempt to "try to motivate yourself by saying, 'I should do this or that'" (Burns, 1980, p. 37). "I've never been a scholar. I'm an administrator—a people person." This kind of cognitive distortion narrowly defines the role of the scholar.

9. *Labeling and mislabeling* create "a completely negative self-image based on your errors" (Burns, 1980, p. 38). "He's good at relating to people in the doctoral program because his dad was a rabbi" is a kind of labeling. "I tried teaching in a very organized way, sticking to the syllabus word-for-word, giving students an agenda and summaries of each class but teaching this way is for geeks" is an example of mislabeling.

10. *Personalization* confuses "influence with control over others" (Burns, 1980, p. 39). "I'll never forgive myself for saying what I did to one of the students in the master's course I taught as part of my doctoral fellowship. He just got on my nerves, and I let him have it in front of the whole class."

All of these cognitive distortions had me paying interest on a debt that I didn't owe and in the process wasting personal and professional resources that could have been better allocated elsewhere in my doctoral program and life. I keep an abbreviated list of these ten distortions in my mind to help me in everyday living. There are some times when I simply withdraw to a quiet place where I can think through my feelings and behavior using the list of cognitive fallacies.

Strategy 4: Have healthy ways of dealing with stress. (See Brubaker and Williams, 2010, pp. 98–111).

Stress originally referred to the engineering field and the structural damage from too much strain. The term was popularized in the early part of the twentieth century in the mental health area and had a negative connotation associated with excessive work, fatigue, and the like (Vanslyke-Briggs, 2010, p. 34).

Stress can, however, simply be a natural part of living, and work to your advantage as long as it doesn't harm you physically. "When it does become problematic, however, is when the stress is long term, ongoing, and results in negative physical and mental outcomes" (Vanslyke-Briggs, 2010, pp. 34–35). It is also true that what is stressful to one person may not be to another.

Stress is frequently caused by the fear of loss of control. Anger and anxiety often go hand in hand with this fear. Depression, sometimes of a spiraling kind, may also be part of the equation. Some doctoral students who have struggled with math classes in the past go through this in taking statistics classes.

What options do you have as a doctoral student in relating to stress? The first step is to locate the source of the stress. Vanslyke-Briggs suggests that a stress journal or diary that identifies what events took place prior to your stressful reaction and its manifestation can be helpful. "Was it physical such as a backache, psychological/emotional such as a crying jag or rage outburst, or was it social such as an avoidance of colleague gatherings" (Vanslyke-Briggs, 2010, p. 37)?

Second, you can sometimes eliminate or certainly minimize sources of stress. It was clear to one doctoral student during the first meeting of his program planning committee that one member of the committee, a non-tenured, recently hired assistant professor, didn't want to be there and only reluctantly signed off on the program of study. One thing that seemed to bother the committee member was that a favorite course he taught, an elective, was not on the program of study.

The student, stressed out about this matter, especially because the department had a history of planning committee members continuing to serve on the dissertation committee, met with his advisor, a respected full professor. With the blessing of the student, the advisor said he would take care of this problem by replacing the committee member with a more supportive tenured professor. This was done and the source of stress for the doctoral student was eliminated.

Another doctoral student had a source of stress that could be minimized but not eliminated. She shared with us her perfectionist tendencies, something that caused her tremendous stress in choosing a dissertation topic. A long meeting with her dissertation advisor eliminated several topics as the student simply didn't have the resources to adequately research them. The advisor then suggested that the two remaining topics were both excellent choices thus minimizing the student's stress.

During a second session with his advisor the student clearly had more passion for one topic rather than the other. The student was then stressed out as to the enormity of the dissertation project. His advisor helped the student view the dissertation as a number of "chunks" with no one perfect place to start.

Once the student began the work that needed to be done she and her advisor were off and running and the dissertation was finished in three semesters. The advisor had become a mentor who helped the doctoral student understand that her dissertation was to be viewed as a number of tasks rather than an overwhelming perfect object.

Third, you can deal with stress by developing new habits or returning to habits that you have set aside. The most common example of this shared by our doctoral students is to identify "go-to" activities that will be healthy physically and emotionally for ourselves and others. Two friends in doctoral study decided to join a health club they visited early in the morning four days a week.

Another student said, "Half an hour on the stationary bike while reading an interesting book gives me a fresh start to each day." One student decided that she would spend time out doors, even for very brief periods of time, to clear her mind and relieve her stress.

The arts afford opportunities to drop out and relax from the stress of doctoral study. A student said that she and a friend serve as ushers at a nearby university so that they can attend operas, plays, musicals, symphony concerts, and operettas free of charge. They also do this for athletic events.

All of these suggestions speak to the need for a balance between doctoral student activities and the rest of your life. Such a balance is not easy to achieve, but even a measure of balance is worth the effort. You can remind yourself that being called Dr. makes all of this worthwhile.

Your goal of earning a doctorate will depend on your sense of self efficacy— "I can do it!" You will see in the remainder of this book that four things are instrumental in your efficacy of self. First, you will establish habits and master skills like critical thinking, critiquing, researching and writing. (See appendix C, "The Power of Critique.")

Second, you will look to others who have been successful in getting their doctoral degrees. They will serve as exemplars who give you backstage information on what it takes to do well in the program. Third, you will build a support system, such as professors, advisors, committee members, and fellow students. Avoid negative people who will pull you down and steal your resources. Fourth, maintain a positive view that will motivate and inspire you.

We will return to the distinction between outer curriculum and inner curriculum on occasion in the remainder of the book. Your awareness of this distinction and efforts you make to reconcile it will pay rich dividends as you move forward to successfully complete your doctorate.

INFORMATION GATHERING
AND SELF-REFLECTION ACTIVITIES

We conclude this chapter with a discussion of ways to systematically record what you experience, your inner curriculum, as you make your way through the doctoral program. We are reminded of the Hansel and Gretel fairy tale of German origin in the Brothers Grimm publication of 1812.

The young brother and sister, children of a woodcutter and his wife, were left by their parents in the woods so there would be two fewer mouths to feed. Hansel gathered white pebbles and dropped them along the path as his parents led the children into the woods. The children easily made their way home the next day following the pebbles.

The children are then taken into the woods a second time by their parents with Hansel marking the trail with bread crumbs, but birds eat the crumbs leaving the trail unmarked. The children are lost in the woods, they are confronted by a witch, they escape from her and discover precious jewels, and are saved by a swan who takes them across the water to their home. Their mother has died but their father, devastated by the loss of his children is delighted upon their return after which they live happily ever after.

Many, if not most doctoral students, like Hansel with his bread crumbs, reach the dissertation stage and have no enduring plan for gathering and organizing reflections and other data. Some don't even have such a plan in place while researching and writing the dissertation.

A few of our students still use hand written notes on three by five cards, easily carried around in a pocket or purse. These cards can then be shuffled and reshuffled according to themes or categories that meet the student's purposes. Other students use electronic devices, such as computers, cell phones and iPads that allow them to cut, copy, and paste their ideas. Word master document files help organize ideas and feelings.

Recorded audio files are another electronic tool that can then be transcribed for further use in research and writing, particularly at the dissertation stage. Some students use photos from cell phones to document the gathering of reflections and other data throughout the doctoral program, especially at the dissertation stage. This pictorial approach lends itself to poster presentations at conventions. Graphs, such as the one in the beginning of this book, can also be constructed to trace student progress in the doctoral program and/or dissertation journey.

It is wise to create a file in which you enter e-mail messages from interactions you have with people throughout the program. *We also urge you to enter as many things as you can in the words of those you encounter.* The authenticity of these remarks will be clear to those who read and hear them.

The confidence you gain from having a system for gathering and organizing reflections and other data throughout the doctoral program in general and the dissertation in particular will lead to hopefulness and optimism you need to finish the degree in fine fashion.

We now turn to three major steps (and chapter titles) you will take to completing your degree: Obtaining and Maintaining Graduate Assistantships and Internships; Comprehensive Exams; and Researching and Writing the Dissertation.

Chapter 4

Graduate Assistantships and Internships

The secret to success in school and in life is *meaningful work*—"the miracle of meaningful work."

—Malcolm Gladwell (2008, p. 269)

As John Dewey pointed out eons ago, there are two kinds of Knowing: Knowledge we have gained on a conceptual level, and knowledge based on concrete experience, which becomes part of your psychological bloodstream.

—Seymour Sarason (2002, p. 60)

The great teachers fill you up with hope and shower you with a thousand reasons to embrace all aspects of life.

—Pat Conroy (2002, p. 63)

Many of you will have the opportunity to be Graduate Assistants (GAs) and/ or Interns. Graduate assistantships may pay several thousand dollars a year and also include a tuition waiver. This waiver can be a significant amount of money for out-of-state students. A few of you will receive fellowships that include tuition waivers and basic living expenses. Your fellowship may place you in the role of research assistant and/or teaching assistant for one or more semesters or quarters of your doctoral study.

Internships are usually off-campus, and doctoral students, unlike most master's students, will likely be paid for being interns. A doctoral student in a counseling program, for example, may have an internship that involves counseling in a clinical health setting. Or a student may hold a research position as an assistant to the coordinator of school counselors in a school district.

Successfully completing graduate assistantships and/or internship experiences will tell interested employers that you can do the kind of research, writing, administrative leadership, and teaching they may be looking for in a new hire. Each doctoral student's job description in the role of graduate assistant or intern will have its own uniqueness, depending on what the person in charge of the assignment has in mind and your own interests and abilities. (See appendix H, "Identifying the Traits of Outstanding Leaders Encountered During My Doctoral Program.")

GRADUATE ASSISTANTSHIPS

Most universities with doctoral programs give stipends for two kinds of responsibilities. Those with research duties are Research Assistants (RAs). Those with teaching duties are Teaching Assistants (TAs). Some administrative tasks may be part of these assistantships. Interaction with faculty is expected. Graduate assistants are required to be full-time graduate students in most doctorate-granting institutions.

Graduate assistants receive a financial stipend and usually get a tuition scholarship. They sometimes join faculty in receiving a discount on books from the university bookstore. They may also receive health insurance. Non-native speakers of English who obtain teaching assistantships are frequently expected to score at least a 3.0 on the *Oral English Proficiency Test* (OEPT) or a 500 on the *Test of English as a Foreign Language* (TOEFL). These test the spoken language skills of non-native speakers of English.

The following snapshot will give you an idea of what a Research Assistant did and learned from a year-long graduate assistantship.

Snapshot 4.1

What I Really Learned as a Research Assistant

My coursework was completed when I received an invitation to become a Research Assistant with a prominent sociologist at the university. He was known for getting doctoral students involved in his heavily funded research projects. He had the reputation of being a mentor who was loyal to doctoral students who worked for him. Those who were mentored by him received good job offers by universities upon their graduation.

I wasn't sure that I wanted to accept the assistantship because I thought it would take time away from my dissertation research and writing, but my advisor said that I could get a dissertation topic and support for research design and the like from the experience. I was offered one of two assistantships awarded to doctoral students who were expected to get a social science research and development project off the ground.

The purpose of the project was to prepare curriculum materials grounded in the social sciences for high school social studies teachers. Writers of the grant proposal wanted to bring breadth from the social sciences to a high school social studies curriculum that was focused on history and civics.

The research assistantship gave me the opportunity to closely observe the leadership style and personality of this prominent sociologist. He was a seasoned scholar who described himself as a sociologist of education rather than an educational sociologist. I quickly discovered that this distinction on his part meant that his Ph.D. was in sociology, not education, and he felt this difference in orientation made an important difference. This introduced me to some of the distinctions university scholars make with regard to issues in their disciplines. I was beginning to learn the game and the score.

This sociologist and project director was not only a scholar, but he was also devoted to social justice issues in general and the civil rights movement in particular. I found it very interesting in spending a good deal of time with him that he was not especially articulate verbally, often slurring his speech so that I had to listen carefully to understand him, but this did not get in the way of his being recognized as a first-rate scholar.

I found it instructive that strengths in some areas, such as research, writing and mentoring, could compensate for weaknesses in other areas. This was one of many lessons I learned from my assistantship that was not in textbooks.

The research project called for a number of well-known social scientists to visit our campus so that we could identify how concepts and methodologies from their social science disciplines could be translated into terms useful in the high school social studies curriculum. I volunteered to take these scholars to restaurants in town at the end of our work days. This gave me the opportunity to engage in conversations with nationally recognized experts about their research, writing, teaching, and relationships with colleagues and doctoral students.

One of these social scientists, for example, said that I would be wise after getting my doctorate not to be an editor of books as it was a thankless job that would work against my getting promotion and tenure. He also advised me to be a single author of major articles and first author of co-authored articles whenever possible.

He told me a story about taking his first co-authored book to his mother over vacation. Her first response was "Why aren't you the first author?" His final word of advice to me was to begin as an assistant professor in a research university as administrators would give me time off from teaching to research and write.

On one occasion, three visiting scholars helped me push my Volkswagen out of a snow bank in front of a restaurant. When I met these scholars at conferences and conventions after my graduation, we laughed at some of the good times we had together. In a sense I felt like I was in a "club" with these scholars, even though I was certainly a neophyte.

They were examples of who I hoped to be as my career developed (Brubaker, 2010, pp. 313–317.) I discussed this matter with one of these scholars, and he told me that I was involved in *anticipatory socialization*. I was beginning to play the anticipated role of a professor before I actually held the position. I found it interesting that I was learning the language of sociology outside of the university classroom.

I also learned a good deal of backstage information about the discretionary power of researchers in doing research. I observed how some marginal data were discounted or discarded by a research team challenged with making these decisions. This was also the case with the interpretation of data we did consider. Members of the research team sometimes laughed about the discretionary power they held.

It was as a research assistant that I began to build networks that helped me with my research and writing. My fellow doctoral students in the research complex where I worked sharpened my dissertation research design, suggested ways in which tables, graphs and charts could display information, and connected me with educators in schools who identified my research population.

We frequently gathered on Friday afternoons to celebrate the end of the work week, share stories about our progress on dissertations, and pick each other up when we were down. It was in my research assistantship that I discovered the importance of community once again.

There is a caveat that should be added to our discussion of research assistantships. The work is very demanding and intense at times, due in large measure to the fact that the professor who has written the grant proposal and is heading the project has a stake in ensuring the success of the research and writing effort. This can work to your advantage if you get your dissertation research from involvement with the project, as was the case with the previous snapshot. Unlike most teaching assistantships, there can be a direct connection between being a research assistant and your dissertation project.

If, however, your research "boss" on the project is also your dissertation advisor, you will not be able to separate these two roles. On occasion your "boss"/advisor may be cranky and irritable. As one research assistant said, "I learned to deal with this primarily by keeping my distance and not trying to be too 'chummy.'" (Thomas & Brubaker, 2001, p. 10.) The doctoral student achieved this in part by addressing his advisor/project director as Dr. or Professor at all times, something that also conveyed respect.

In the previous snapshot, the professor who headed the research project was not the doctoral student's dissertation advisor and was not a member of the student's planning or dissertation committee. In fact, the student never took a course from the sociologist who headed the research project. This is another example of how you, the doctoral student, can learn a good deal from professors who you never had courses from and never served on your planning or dissertation committee.

There is another possible advantage in taking a research assistantship. In a tight job market some research assistants stay on as paid researchers in the research project after graduation, thus avoiding unemployment.

Teaching Assistantships may also be a valuable part of doctoral study. It can be useful to shadow and observe other teaching assistants before you begin in this role. A mentor can also play an important role in making your teaching assistantship a success, as can other teaching assistants who are both competent and caring.

An obvious advantage in being a teaching assistant is that the experience you acquire while helping undergraduates can work to your advantage if you want to go into college or university teaching after you finish your degree. Having been a teaching assistant will also look good on your record when you are hunting for a position that includes teaching duties.

There are various levels of responsibility and pay in teaching assistantships. Frequently, students are encouraged to teach voluntarily with various professors who share their interests or where the student may learn new teaching techniques and styles. This can be an excellent opportunity for a student to observe a quality instructor and receive supervision in their own fledgling teaching practices. Most often, these positions are unpaid and the responsibilities are fewer as the professor remains the *instructor-of-record*, or the official teacher recognized and paid by the university.

Other teaching assistantships are paid positions and are more frequently in undergraduate courses. Many departments have realized the benefits of giving graduate students this type of teaching experience while increasing enrollment in lucrative ways. If the graduate student is the instructor of record, she or he is likely paid for their services.

These positions are the most coveted as they, like the research positions, include many financial perks. Additionally, these positions look attractive to potential employers (universities) who see that the student has assumed full responsibility for the class, and there are often instructor evaluations associated with this experience that can be shared with interested employers.

There is, however, a downside to being a teaching assistant. It takes a lot of time, as undergraduates can be quite demanding, especially in this electronic age. It takes a good deal of time to prepare for your class(es), and reading students' writing also takes time. You may be expected to attend weekly meetings with other teaching assistants, something that draws on your resources (Thomas & Brubaker, 2001, p. 9.)

The following snapshots move you, the reader, backstage into the life of a doctoral student in the role of teaching assistant. The first snapshot has the teaching assistant in a traditional setting, whereas the second one has the same teaching assistant in an online setting.

Snapshot 4.2

What I Learned as a Teaching Assistant in Traditional Settings

As a graduate student, teaching courses on my own was one of the most frightful and empowering experiences of all that I had completed to date. I knew that I was going to become a faculty member following my graduation and realized that I would need to learn how to teach. Unfortunately, like many programs, mine did not offer any courses on class instruction, so I had to ask a lot of questions from professors in the department and from the university's instructional support services.

There were many lessons I gained from that experience: having to prepare my own lectures, develop a syllabus, facilitate students' crises, and address major code of conduct violations. One of the biggest learning experiences came when a student began to challenge me in the classroom, questioning my knowledge about the topic of our current lecture, substance abuse.

Even though I received years of training in the classroom and in my clinical practice on this topic, I found myself dumbfounded, unable to answer the questions he had for me on this topic. It was the intensity of these questions that bothered me the most, almost as if I was being attacked. After class, when my head stopped spinning, I came to the realization that I did not need to know everything in the class and that despite my preparations, there would always be something beyond my information base. Interestingly, this was only the first lesson of this experience.

The bigger lesson occurred during the following week, when I came back to class to share my realization. Quite frankly, I shared with the class that I would be on this learning journey with them at many points, and while I had a lot of information, so did they. And sometimes none of us would know the answer and we could find out together.

At the end of class, the student who had challenged me came up and began to share that a family member of hers relapsed on crack cocaine over the past couple of weeks and that she was scared and did not know where to turn. She wanted my help. Remaining in the role of instructor, I quickly assisted her in getting connected to the counseling center and some other support services in town.

What I realized was that this student was, in fact, testing me the week prior to see if I was able to help her. Was I capable as a clinician? Some times things are not always as they seem on the surface. She did not want to attack me. She wanted help. Fortunately, I was able to show in and out of the classroom that I did not have to be the one to provide all of the answers.

Snapshot 4.3

The Online Teaching Assistantship

When I started as a facilitator (teaching assistant) in an online course, I thought I was in a foreign country. I had never taken an online course before, but I had used Blackboard, the school's online platform, as an on-campus student. Online courses were never very highly regarded in my undergraduate program, as they were primarily offered by unaccredited programs, seemingly to make a quick buck. But now, they are everywhere, so I thought I would give it a chance. I am really glad that I did.

Most of my work has come as a facilitator of discussion boards in an asynchronous format. (Students can participate at their leisure throughout the week instead of at the same fixed classroom time.) I have also helped to grade assignments, offer technical support for live chat sessions, and created modules for the class. One of the most amazing things I have learned is how much students disclose with one another and the class in this format. In fact, I have to make sure they don't say too much that they might regret later on.

I still prefer the human contact of the classroom, but I can now see that community can be created in the online environment as well. Also, I am able to interact individually with the students in my group in ways that I would not have normally done in a face-to-face class.

It has been interesting to see how technology can be used not only to instruct, but also to verify the authenticity of an assignment. When a student once plagiarized, I had to learn how to navigate through the University's Code of Conduct and the procedures that followed. It was interesting to see how these rules were implemented with online students who lived hundreds of miles away from campus. I feel like my eyes have opened up to a whole different world, and even if I do not teach an online course in my first faculty position, I hope to use some of the technology to better my on-campus courses.

In total, there are many great experiences that can be learned as a teaching assistant. It is always good to remember that your departments and universities have needs to both train you but also to maintain (or increase) enrollment at a low cost to their budgets. Sometimes these interests can be in conflict with one another, so it is up to you to advocate for yourself and create the best experiences for your long-term interests.

As you determine what types of experiences are best for you, it can be helpful to think about your ideal position following your graduation. Do you plan to work as a faculty member in a research extensive university? In that case, you might want to focus on research assistantships and experiences.

If you plan to serve in a teaching-focuses university or college, you would be better served by attending to teaching assistantships. Likely, you will do both, but you always have the option to increase your focus on one area or the other. Of course, there are many who will forgo taking a faculty position altogether, instead seeking a professional position outside of academia. Our next section, Internships, will be a critical area of concern for this type of student.

INTERNSHIPS

Internships can play an important role in your doctoral study. The experience you gain can introduce you to what it is like to be employed in a field of work in general and a particular job within that field. Your choice of a specific internship will also let future employers know that you have made an informed decision that has given you special expertise. One intern, for example, did internships with the homeless population and persons with addictions, areas of expertise that led to a university position in the Midwest.

Your internship will give you a backstage view of this profession and those who work in it. You will also be given an orientation to a profession and job. This will afford you an opportunity to assess the kinds of leaders and colleagues who work in this profession. The more inquisitive you are, the more information you will have about your own career path.

You will not only gain experience from your internship, but you will also have an early start and possibly higher starting salary in the event that you choose this kind of work as you begin your career. Time after time doctoral graduates tell us that their internship(s) led to job opportunities.

The following snapshot helps us understand what one doctoral intern learned during the internship experience.

Snapshot 4.4

An Introduction to a New World of Work

My doctoral internship experience was quite different from my master's internship experience. While a master's student, I was most concerned about meeting licensure requirements and becoming versed in the standards and practices of a mental health counselor. In essence, I targeted the most competitive of clinical positions where I could learn from "the best." As a doctoral student, I found myself gravitating towards a more unique experience, one that was related to my research interests and one that I could eventually become among "the best."

Having volunteered with a group serving homeless camp communities, I found a clinician working for the county housing authority who was in charge of a unique program providing housing and social services to formerly homeless individuals and families, now living in their own apartments. I knew I wanted to develop my expertise in this area, so I inquired within my doctoral program and found out how to make this an approved internship site.

As you could guess, I learned an incredible amount about the experience of transitioning from the camps to housing. All of my clients had severe mental illnesses and most were addicted to mind-altering chemicals. They were amazing teachers who were willing to share their lives with me and allow me to provide assistance where possible. Their struggles with various social systems provided the inspiration for my dissertation work, an exploration of the barriers to substance abuse and mental health services.

This internship was also important as it helped me make many connections in the area so that I could collect data for my dissertation. I began to understand the "system" as both a provider and through the eyes of my clients. My connections allowed me to gain access to both the agencies where formerly homeless people lived, but also to the camps and public places where my clients had once lived and still had a network of friends.

In addition, my passion for my topic was easily supplied by my care for these clients. All of these factors played an important role in my successful completion of my dissertation as well as the integration of my overall doctoral experience.

GRADUATE STUDENT UNIONS

Labor unions that represent graduate students exist in some public colleges and universities in the United States and Canada where state collective bargaining laws are in place. Bargaining rights under the Federal Taft-Harley Act do not apply to state and local government employees. "The suitability of collective bargaining for graduate students is the contested issue" (Cavell, 2000, p. 1).

Are graduate students primarily students or employees? Unions argue in the affirmative, particularly in hard economic times when universities use more teaching assistants as a source of cheap labor and hire fewer tenured faculty members in line positions. If you are a teaching assistant, your income will probably be taxed on a W-2 form required for employment income rather than on a 1042-S form for scholarships.

Opponents of collective bargaining for graduate students, largely faculty and administrators, argue that "students work as part of their training or financial aid packages, and this experience supplements their education" (Cavell, 2000, p. 2). They say that union membership in general and strikes are disruptive thus interfering with the teaching and learning process. They add that unions have frozen the amount of money paid to graduate assistants due to confrontations with those who hire them.

A key question concerns the nature of universities. Is the university primarily a community or a corporation? Some argue that the trend is for university presidents and chancellors to have backgrounds that are more like Chief Executive Officers (CEOs) and less like researchers and scholars. If this is the case, it follows that graduate assistants are treated more like a cheap labor force rather than teachers and researchers at the beginning of their careers.

It is interesting to note the history of Graduate-Student Unions in the United States. The oldest graduate assistants' union that still exists is the Teaching Assistant's Association at the University of Wisconsin-Madison, an organization that settled its first contract in 1970 after a four week strike. During that year the graduate student instructors at the University of Michigan formed the Graduate Employees' Organization, which won its first contract in 1975.

Considerable unionization activity in the 1980s has continued to this day. You may receive additional information about this activity from two sources: the National Association of Graduate-Professional Students (NAGPS) [http://www.nagps.org/] and the Coalition of Graduate Employee Unions (CGEU) [htty://www.CGEU.org/].

The challenge for you, a Graduate Assistant seeking a doctorate, is to do your homework in order to find out more about these issues and how they can affect you. The contexts in which you are getting your degree, such as your doctoral committee, your dissertation committee, your department and your school or college, must be understood and related to in light of your priorities.

As usual, there is a dialectic of forces you must accommodate: What is the status quo? What should be the case? And, what can be done given your core values and sources of power? Trusted doctoral graduates, veteran doctoral students in your program and others may be helpful to you as you negotiate the territory. (See appendix E, "Dealing with Contradictions in a Doctoral Program.")

Chapter 5

Comprehensive Examinations

The comps gave me a chance to pull together everything that I learned up to that point. I began to see a coherence in my work that I hadn't seen before.

—Lawrence H. Simon (December 18, 2010)

Wisdom is what lasts after an experience ends.

—Joan Chittister (2008, p. 124)

I've learned that people will forget what you said, people will forget what you did, but people will never forget how you made them feel.

—Maya Angelou (December 2009, p. 27)

Comprehensive exams are a major part of most doctoral programs. As indicated by the word "comprehensive," they cover a broad base of material. The exams vary a good deal from one university to another. The first place to begin your search for information on comprehensive exams, or comps as they are usually called, is the Graduate School Catalogue. General guidelines for the exams are usually found in this catalogue with more specific information in materials distributed by your department's doctoral program coordinator.

Although many doctoral programs require you to satisfactorily complete all of your coursework before taking the exams, some programs allow you to take the exams after three-fourths or so of your coursework is done. One advantage of this is that you can formally move straight into your dissertation after coursework is completed, thus keeping the momentum and not having a long pause after you are through with your classes.

A second advantage of taking the comps early is that residency is required for taking the exam, thus saving you a semester's tuition and fees if you can handle taking comps and coursework at the same time. In one university where we taught, doctoral students had not read the Graduate School catalogue on this matter of taking the comps early and didn't consider taking advantage of this opportunity until we brought it to their attention. Some students boldly stepped forward, accepted responsibility on this matter and graduated early. (See appendix D, "The 'Table Manners' of Doctoral Student Leadership.")

In many doctoral programs you formally become a doctoral candidate after you pass your comprehensive examinations. Passing the exams is your ticket that says you are prepared by your coursework to move on to the dissertation stage of the doctoral program.

The purpose of the comprehensive examinations is not always clear to faculty or doctoral students. As one student said, "Why should I be tested a second time for material in courses where I have already passed examinations and successfully written papers?" What then are some of the stated reasons for the comprehensive exams?

First, students are given the opportunity to integrate knowledge they have acquired in their coursework and experiences like internships, teaching assistantships, research assistantships, and attendance at conferences and conventions. This purpose for the exams, if it becomes central to the selection of questions and assessment formats, can be a valuable learning experience for the student. You will note this in the first header quote in this chapter.

A second reason for the exams is to weed out students with research and writing problems, after which students with such issues either work on these skills and take the comps a second time or decide to drop out of the program. Most programs don't give students more than two chances to pass the exams.

One would think that this sorting process would have taken place during the coursework phase of the program, but sometimes it has not. It would seem to follow that students at risk are those most anxious about taking comprehensive examinations, but this is not necessarily the case. Comps are anxiety provoking, in part because questions of any kind can be asked and students are wary of what they call "curveball questions"—unseen and therefore unexpected questions.

Many doctoral programs divide the comps into two parts, written and oral. Other programs only have a written or oral exam, usually the former rather than the latter. When there are two parts to the exams, the oral is a defense of the written exams but questions are not limited to the student's writing. There are some programs where the dissertation proposal, usually in a brief general format, becomes a part of the discussion.

Questions for the written exams are sometimes constructed by the entire department or a representative group from the department, with the same questions given to all doctoral students who take the exams at a particular time. Other doctoral programs have questions written by the student's program committee, often three members and an advisor. Students may or may not be asked to suggest questions. Questions may be known or not known to students before the exams are given. A general field of study as well as an area of specialization may be tested.

The exams may or may not be "open book." In some programs students are allowed to write their exams at a place of their own choosing, often where they live or at the university library. In other programs students are assigned a place at the university. Time to write may or may not be regulated and monitored.

Students are sometimes given a reading list that may or may not be added to by them. More traditional and current references will probably be included. Some professors will have an unrealistically long reading list. You will need to prioritize the books on their list.

The following snapshot will take you backstage into the experience one doctoral student had with the comprehensive exams.

Snapshot 5.1

Making It Through My Written and Oral Comps

My doctoral program chair was also my dissertation advisor, and she was very competent in both roles. When I asked her about preparation for the comprehensive exams, she told me her views in straight-forward language. "You have already demonstrated you are ready to take your comps, or I would have held you back until you were ready."

She continued, "You write well, and you have done excellent work in your courses. We have also put together a program committee that is very supportive of you, and they think you are ready to write your comps. You will want to speak to each of them about their questions. Remember, you are allowed to bring notes to your exams, and you will write a half day for each of the four professors on your committee."

She added: "I believe that you do not need to be questioned and assessed a second time in the same way you were in your courses. The comps, from my point of view, are an excellent opportunity to transition from coursework to your dissertation. You have a good general idea of what your dissertation will be since you are building on the work you did as a Graduate Research Assistant in the research project I headed. My questions will be focused on what you learned in your research courses, your dissertation proposal course, and your experiences in our research project."

She then raised the question, "What did you learn from these three things that will be helpful to you in constructing your dissertation research design? Secondly, how will you organize your literature search? For example, what will be the key indicators or themes for your search, and what methods will you use to do your search? Be as specific as possible."

The second member of my committee, a professor whose background was in the philosophy of education, gave me the following study question: "Go through your notes and books you read in my class and ask yourself how they speak to what you think should be the purpose for the comprehensive exams." This study threw me at first but I found it interesting and used it in going through my materials I had saved from his class as well as the books we had read for the class.

The third committee member was from my cognate field in sociology. She handed me a list of 50 study questions that members of the sociology department had prepared. She asked me what sociology courses I had taken and said that she would choose four questions that related to these courses. I reviewed this list and identified 30 questions that were obviously related to the courses I had taken.

I tend to be a perfectionist, and because of this and the high anxiety I had about the comps, I took extensive notes in preparing for the 30 questions. I said to myself, "This is the last time in my life that I am going to overstudy for questions like this." I was definitely prepared for the four questions that I received.

The fourth member of my committee treated the comp process with a kind of benign indifference. He was a year or so from retirement and asked me to give him two questions that he could share with the committee chair. I complied and answered these questions with no difficulty.

My program chair scheduled the dean's conference room and the dean's secretary, who monitored the comps, occasionally stopped by the room during the two days to ask me how I was doing and if I wanted some water.

A month later my committee chair and committee members held my oral defense of the written comps. My chair advised me to answer questions briefly, to the point and STOP! She said I should let committee members talk to each other, disagree with each other, or whatever without interfering with this process.

They liked what I had written, gave me a high pass, and said that they looked forward to our next meeting when I would present a dissertation proposal. The only "curve ball" I received was when one committee member asked me what I got out of this whole comp experience. To be honest, I don't remember what I said, but I was glad to get this behind me and move on to the more focused matter of dissertation research and writing.

HOW TO PREPARE FOR YOUR COMPREHENSIVE EXAMS

Although comprehensive exams vary a good deal from one university to another, there are some guidelines that may be helpful to you as you prepare to take the exams. We will refer to the previous snapshot, when appropriate, to illustrate points we wish to make.

Have a productive "can do" attitude. If you view this stage of your doctoral program as an opportunity to integrate your learning experiences up to this point in anticipation of your dissertation, you will not simply see this as jumping over a hurdle. You will instead see this as something you can use in doing dissertation research and writing and in the process occasionally enjoy pulling together your past experiences, such as coursework, your graduate assistantship, internship, and attendance at conferences and conventions. (See appendix C, "The Power of Critique.") The doctoral student in the previous snapshot was fortunate to have an advisor who followed this guideline and chose questions that transitioned the student from coursework to the dissertation.

Support from fellow doctoral students can be helpful as going it alone can be difficult in this anxiety-producing experience. Study groups may give you the company you need at times if others in the group take the process seriously and stay on task. (See appendix F, "Working Alone and Working As a Team Member.") Students who have already experienced comps may also give you advice that is useful. They will sometimes share copies of exams that are especially helpful if you have the same professors they had as questioners.

Be proactive in preparing for the comps. It is up to you to initiate contact with persons who can give you appropriate information about what to study for and how to study for these exams. If your doctoral committee is responsible for formulating questions, make an appointment with each professor to discuss these matters, beginning with your committee chair.

Your taking the initiative will let them know that you take the comps seriously. Don't have an attitude of "I know they are busy and I don't want to bother them." The doctoral student in the previous snapshot was proactive in seeking comp questions and/or advice on how to study for the exam.

Once you begin taking notes and organizing ideas, questions may arise in your mind. (See appendix P, "Note Taking As an Important Part of the

Research and Writing Process.") Feel free to ask professors for more information that will make things clearer for you to move forward. You may address
these questions to committee members and other professors. Intern advisors
and graduate assistants may also be helpful at this point, especially if your
questions deal with the application of ideas in the field.

Stay focused. It is easy to go down blind alleys and overstudy as the student in the previous snapshot did with questions on the sociology study list.
Your mind can have information overload. One way to deal with this is to use
electronic and hard copy ways to highlight key ideas. If you are outlining, you
may leave a large margin on the left side where you can have a brief outline
of important points. In reviewing the page, start with the short outline and go
to the longer outline only when you need more information.

It is understandable, given the natural anxiety you will feel, to say more
than you need to say at the oral defense. The student in the snapshot was
advised by the program chair to answer questions concisely and precisely.
Professors and other like to hear themselves talk. Let them! (See appendix I,
"How Good and Comfortable Are You As a Speaker and Listener?")

As you look at references and other sources, do so with a discerning eye.
Check the dates on these materials. Have an eye out for powerful ideas and
note who the persons are who have these ideas. Google them to learn more
about them so that you can share this information with the exam reader. It is
important to stay current, but it is equally important to identify ideas from the
past that have stood the test of time.

Keep in mind who your audience is and write for them. Your main audience
is the professor who wrote the question(s) for you to answer. It is natural for
this professor to think he or she has special expertise or the question(s) would
not be asked of you. Your recognition of this will be communicated verbally
and non-verbally with your writing and especially at the oral defense. If the
professor you are writing for has published on the subject you are writing
about, cite this professor's research and writing. This is both legitimate and
flattering to the professor.

Your secondary audience is the other professors who read your answers
and attend your oral defense, if there is one. Have a mindset that recog-
nizes their expertise for being chosen to be on the committee to assess
your answers. Your recognition of this will be noted by them. The doctoral
student in the previous snapshot was very focused in his preparation for the
comps.

Write clearly and coherently. Bringing precision to your writing is a creative act. One way to do this is to place your topic sentences, your main ideas,
at the beginning of each paragraph. Supporting material should be related to
this major idea in order to bring coherence to your work. Material that is not

related should simply be deleted. There are times when an especially powerful idea should be italicized or underlined to bring special attention to it.

If you are introducing a term that may not be known to the reader, briefly define it. There is no need to be pedantic by using big words where smaller ones may do. You are intelligent or you wouldn't be at this place in your doctoral program. There is no need to be pompous or arrogant.

Keep in mind the main purpose of the comprehensive examinations. The question your examining committee must answer is, "Has the doctoral student demonstrated that he or she is prepared to enter the dissertation stage?" When the answer is "Yes," you will have the satisfaction of knowing that your committee is clearly behind you and will continue to support you as you move forward to the dissertation stage of your doctoral program.

Chapter 6

Dissertation Research and Writing

Is this a valid educational activity? Yes, it is, ladies and gentlemen, because this is a writing class and everything is grist to our mill.

—Frank McCourt (2005, p. 225)

A word can change the atmosphere of a sentence or paragraph.

—Frank McCourt (2005, p. 222)

An English professor at Harvard College said that "the luck of the conception" is the key to writing any fine book, short story or the like."

—Tracy Kidder (2006, p. 23)

My advisor/mentor taught me the importance of the conception of the dissertation project.

—Lauren Shure (September 4, 2010 interview)

It was in Philadelphia, while working as a columnist for the *Philadelphia Inquirer*, that I had an epiphany. The challenge isn't to figure out how to write, I realized, but why. Without a mission and a sense of whom you write for, you aren't worth reading.

—Steve Lopez (2008, p. 51)

We're getting to the point where our ability to collect information far exceeds our ability to analyze it.

—Brent Scowcroft, as told to Andrea Mitchell, *Talking Back* (2005, p. 343)

Working on your dissertation can be one of the most challenging and reward-ing parts of a doctoral program. In previous stages of the doctoral program your program advisor and professors made many decisions for you. In fact, they framed how you were expected to meet their requirements for passing courses, participating in internships, and the like.

With the dissertation "the ball is in your court" and *you are expected to frame this document* in your own way. The third and fourth header quotes at the beginning of this chapter refer to this as the conception of the writ-ing project. Our doctoral students find it helpful to be reminded that we use frameworks all of the time in our decision making. For example, it is Sunday night, and you are on your way home from an out-of-town vacation. You decide to stop at a supermarket near your home to pick up milk, bread, cereal, and the like. You quickly and efficiently know where to go in the supermarket in order to get these items. And, of equal or greater importance, you know where *not* to go in this supermarket, thus saving you a good deal of time.

All of this is the result of planning done by supermarket managers and others. Foods and other items are grouped according to large organizing concepts, such as dairy products, bakery products, and cereals. There are sub-concepts within each of the larger organizing concepts that help you narrow your choices even more.

The traditional dissertation format also sets markers and boundaries: Chapter 1, Introduction; Chapter 2, Review of the Literature; Chapter 3, Research Methodologies; Chapter 4, Presentation of Findings; Chapter 5, Analysis of Findings; and Chapter 6, Summary, Conclusions, and Recom-mendations. (See appendix L, "Example of a Traditional Table of Contents for a Dissertation".) There are subconcepts within each chapter. There are many variations of this traditional dissertation format, but you will usually find elements from the traditional format in them in some way.

The fact that organizing concepts are basic and essential in dissertations has important implications for you as you do your research and writing. You prepare the way for this research and writing by searching for concepts that will help you frame your dissertation in a way that will meet your needs. This is the place where your uniqueness comes into play in framing the disserta-tion. Where will these concepts come from?

The first header quote in this chapter, by Frank McCourt, reminds us that *everything is grist to our mill as writers*. Much to your surprise, you will often discover concepts in the most unexpected places: radio programs such as National Public Radio, television programs, movies, newspapers, magazines, and informal conversations. These places, along with academic sources, such as research articles, books, lectures, convention programs, and the like, will be most helpful in identifying concepts.

A dissertation student recently shared with us her discovery of a concept, *conspiracy of silence*, while listening to a storyteller on National Public Radio. The concept was used to describe how a student who was disciplined at school didn't tell his parents about his infraction, knowing full well that his abusive father would punish him even more. He also was quite sure that the assistant principal at school wouldn't tell the student's father as the assistant principal knew the father was abusive. There was a tacit or understood conspiracy of silence in effect.

The student's dissertation focused on the importance of *voice* for women in school system superintendencies. She immediately identified *conspiracy of silence* as a concept she could use in her dissertation research and writing. She explored many and varied ways in which some women superintendents and their constituents entered into conspiracies of silence.

We have spent some time on this matter of framing a dissertation as our students have told us that this is one of the two or three most important things they learned from us in doing dissertation research and writing. Your challenge throughout the dissertation research and writing process is to decide what you will include in your framework and what you will leave out. When your framework feels right to you, you will be like the potter at the wheel for you will know that the shape of what you have created, the dissertation, gives you immeasurable pleasure.

SOURCES OF GUIDANCE

You are now at the place in your doctoral program where you have *formally* entered the dissertation stage. You are in a position to identify potential sources of help and the advantages and limitations of each. These sources are academic advisors, fellow doctoral students, experts outside of your own department or university, your own experiences, personal and professional networking, and professional literature.

Dissertation Advisors

It is at the dissertation stage that your advisor's role is of paramount importance, for this person's credibility is on the line when any questions about your research and writing are raised. You will need to have your advisor's approval for your own research and writing decisions. You and your advisor have to be on the same page at the same time in defending what you have done. Time and time again we have experienced situations, particularly during the formal dissertation defense, where the dissertation advisor steps in to articulate support for the research and writing of the dissertation student. A sigh of relief is on the student's face when this happens.

On those occasions when committee members trust the expertise of the academic advisor, all is well. When such trust does not exist, chaos and disarray bring the dissertation defense to a screeching halt. The dissertation student can only move forward again after regrouping and constructing a plan for addressing the problem(s) raised. The following snapshot illustrates the kind of "dance" that often occurs in the process of choosing a first-rate dissertation advisor.

Snapshot 6.1

Choosing the Right Dissertation Advisor

I was taking a class with Dr. David Purpel when I was accepted into the doctoral program. I knew right away that I would like for him to chair my dissertation committee. He did not readily agree to do it. I was concerned that he may not "take me on!" He asked for some time to think about it when I first asked him. In a few weeks he agreed and explained to me that he always took his time to think over the situation before agreeing to such a request since he did not take this matter lightly. He said that if he were to chair my committee, I would definitely complete the program and not end up in the All But the Dissertation (ABD) bin. I would need to follow his lead, do what he asked. It was not easy or quick.

For a year, we met weekly to discuss my progress, my frequent writer/ researcher's block, or for him to critique any additional piece of writing I had completed. Occasionally, our discussions would digress to his resorting to the ultimate wake-up call . . . his shooting me with the dreaded *purple* water-gun he kept "cocked" in his middle desk drawer! What great comic relief that provided when I was overwhelmed or needed to lighten up and gain perspective!

The meetings were sometimes playful, sometimes painful as his feedback was poignant, direct, and oftentimes necessitated my going back to the drawing board and rethinking by reading and reflecting on books or articles he suggested, and then, rewriting. But always, I left those meetings reassured that I was learning and making progress and that, armed with his helpful feedback and guidance, I could make my work more substantive and reflective. I never regretted my choice of him as an advisor and always felt very "special" to have him working with me, and giving so much of his time and concern for me and my work. He was, indeed, a world-class scholar and marvelous man who elevated my level of thinking and contributed appreciably to my capacity to learn, love and live a better life . . . and to help others do the same!

This story, by respected author and professor, Sandra Gupton, makes several important points. She turned to a world-class scholar, David Purpel, to ask him to be her dissertation advisor. This took courage and a willingness to engage in a high level of research and writing on her part. It also took patience in waiting for a response to her invitation as Professor Purpel took the advisor-advisee relationship seriously. [Note that he didn't shy away from his perceived role as advisor/leader and said Sandra would need to follow *his* lead. This wasn't a non-directive counseling session.] In return, he assured her that his students completed their doctoral programs.

Both advisor and advisee honored their commitment to meet once a week, an appreciable amount of time. David Purpel respected Sandra's potential as a scholar in general and writer in particular. He didn't compromise his standards. The dissertation was not simply a hurdle to be jumped over or a hoop to be jumped through. It was a substantive work to be reflected upon and refined. He also respected her as a person. Finally, Sandra Gupton recognized that her advisor made a positive difference *in her life*, not simply in her dissertation research and writing. "Curriculum," for both of them, was life, not simply a course of study to be covered. (See Macdonald, 1977.) In short, there was a good fit between advisor and doctoral student. [Professor Purpel's passing away in 2011 was grieved by all of us but his legacy lives on in former students like Sandra Gupton (Shapiro, 2010, pp. 319–320)].

In some doctoral programs a dissertation advisor is assigned to the student. This takes the responsibility for choosing an advisor away from the student but may not give the student the kind of help needed. In other programs students are expected to engage in discussions with potential advisors. The doctoral student is expected to initiate contact and ask a professor to be a dissertation advisor. When agreement is reached, the advisor and student sign off and their formal relationship is registered with the university.

We should note that there are occasions when the doctoral student and/or dissertation advisor no longer feel there is a good fit to continue their relationship. A change should take place honoring the civilities of candor and respect when this occurs. For example, there is no substitute for face-to-face conversations with the parties concerned in the change. A change in the early stage of dissertation research and writing is easier than in more advanced stages of this process. A change of advisors sometimes happens when it is obvious that another member of the dissertation committee or a new person added to the committee would serve the student better.

In choosing your dissertation advisor, you should be mindful of the fact that this person will be asked by future employers about your promise as a candidate for a position. In some cases the advisor moves to another position and may consider you for future employment. Your advisor will also be in a position to help you get publications into print, including parts or perhaps or all of your dissertation. When all goes well with your advisor, this person may well become your mentor.

It will become obvious to you at the dissertation stage that you can collect valuable information about professors in the pool of potential advisors. What are some of the sources of this information? Faculty members, many of whom you have taken courses from, fellow students, research and teaching assistants, secretaries (executive assistants) and publications by professors can give you valuable information.

Kinds of Information to Collect

The following kinds of information about potential dissertation advisors will be available to you: (a) areas of interest and expertise, (b) advising style, and (c) attitudes about appropriate research topics and research methods.

Areas of interest and expertise on the part of professors are always interesting to investigate. Faculty publications, such as published books and articles, dissertations chaired by faculty members, classes taught by professors and conversations with professors will reveal the passions and talents of potential dissertation advisors. If you don't have a dissertation topic in mind, you will be exploring possible areas of research and writing in a general way. If you do have a dissertation topic in mind, you can rather quickly see if there is a match between a potential dissertation advisor's research interests and your own. You may also find it helpful to read dissertations written by potential advisors.

Dissertation advisors' advising styles vary a good deal, as we have seen in the previous snapshot. Some advisors keep a close watch on students' work whereas others do not. Some advisors want committee members and themselves to receive each chapter of the dissertation as it is written whereas others want to see a complete draft of the dissertation before reacting to it. Availability of an advisor's time is also a matter of considerable importance. Some advisors, such as David Purpel in the previous snapshot, want a good deal of face-to-face time with students whereas others may prefer e-mail and other electronic forms of communication with students.

Your sensitivity to criticism and need for positive affirmation is another factor to consider in choosing a dissertation advisor. Once again, trusted professors and fellow students will probably give you the best feedback on these issues. With regard to advice from professors, you will need to be especially attentive to their non-verbal cues and the tone of their comments about other professors as they are often reluctant to say too much about colleagues on sensitive matters.

Attitudes toward appropriate topics and research methods are of considerable importance to the dissertation student. All professors have certain preferences, indeed biases, as to what constitutes proper research. Some prefer quantitative research, some favor qualitative research, and still others will advocate blended research methodologies. You will often discover their views on these matters in reading their writings. The key to your success in completing your dissertation is a match between your beliefs as to what constitutes appropriate research and the research beliefs held by the dissertation advisor with whom you will work.

The following list of traits of effective dissertation advisors will be useful to you as you decide who to ask to be your dissertation advisor:

- Is well respected by colleagues, students and administrators.
- Is an expert in the field of study your dissertation treats and the research methodology(ies) you wish to use.
- Supports the research problem you have chosen or helps you find a better problem and is flexible, rather than rigid, when appropriate.
- Has the ability to help you with the conception of the project and follows through in advising you to realize this conception by having high but realizable standards. (See the third and fourth header quotes in the beginning of this chapter.)
- Will be available to give verbal and written reactions at the time you need them and will help you set realistic deadlines.
- Is a strong, convincing supporter of advisees and has the courage and ability to defend students in front of other professors, which may be necessary during the research process and particularly at the end when the study is submitted for final examination.
- Gives the kind of emotional support that you need and conveys belief in your ability to move forward with research and writing.
- Does not intrude on your personal life in inappropriate ways.
- Is consistent in giving advice. Does not continually ask for revisions that are to contain new elements. Is not a laid-back micromanager who at the last minute becomes highly prescriptive with a seemingly endless number of changes (Thomas & Brubaker, 2001, p. 60).
- Works amicably with other members of your supervising committee. Helps you select suitable committee members (Thomas & Brubaker, 2008, p. 18.

See appendix J, "A Conversation with Seymour B. Sarason About the Creation and Dynamics of the Dissertation Committee.")

We have focused thus far in our discussion of academic advisors on your formal dissertation advisor, your advisor of record who will guide you through to completion of your doctorate. This person is obviously important to your success. A doctoral graduate we interviewed issues a kind of warning with regard to your relationship with your advisor: "Don't put all of your eggs in one basket. To do so makes you too subjective and dependent on one person. A friend's advisor suddenly left the university and this student was all alone until he was able to develop other relationships with faculty who could help him finish his degree."

You are wise to avail yourself of a universe of opportunities in the dissertation research and writing process that can be used to write a first-rate dissertation. It only remains for you to identify these sources and adopt a proactive stance in order to access them. A positive and professional attitude on your part will be recognized and appreciated by professors. You will by this time have developed a track record that will be recognized by the faculty. (See appendix D, "The 'Table Manners' of Doctoral Student Leadership.")

An immediate and obvious source is your dissertation committee, typically three to five professors you and your dissertation advisor believe will help you achieve your research and writing goals. These professors will advise you on stages of the research and writing process, monitor your progress, assess the final draft of your dissertation, and sign off on forms saying that you have successfully completed the dissertation and degree. If functioning well, they will be your core group of official support.

The most important thing to remember about your dissertation committee is that the committee has its own personality that may differ from your individual relationships with committee members. Their relationships with each other *in the committee setting* are what really matters. When the committee functions *as a team* committed to your successfully completing the doctorate all should be well with problems simply minor issues that can be overcome by people of good will. When a committee does not operate in this way committee members' egos can get out of control and minor issues become major annoyances that threaten your completion of the degree.

It will be up to your dissertation advisor to guide you through the political climate of the university setting so that personal animosities are non-existent or at least minimized in relation to your dissertation committee's work (see appendix J, "A Conversation with Seymour B. Sarason About the Creation and Dynamics of the Dissertation Committee," and appendix E, "Dealing with Contradictions in a Doctoral Program").

We now turn to an issue that can be extremely important, although it is rarely written about in books on dissertation research and writing. This is the professional status of committee members *inside of the university*. Many universities will only *officially* allow full or associate members of the graduate school faculty to chair dissertations. To be a full or associate member of the graduate school faculty means that the professor has applied for and received this status from the graduate school. Full or associate membership is usually predicated by the faculty member having tenure and at least an associate professorship. (Three ranks within the professoriate are assistant, associate, and full professors.) Some graduate school bulletins or catalogs will list faculty members, with those *endorsed* to chair doctoral committees having an (E) after their names.

In some situations, largely when a beginning assistant professor has a special interest and expertise in the subject matter of the dissertation, a non-tenured faculty member will be a co-chair with a full or associate member of the graduate school faculty. In this case the relationship between the co-chairs must be respectful and fully supported by other members of the dissertation committee. It is important that the full or associate member of the graduate school faculty recognize the hard work and expertise of the non-tenured faculty member, especially when the non-tenured faculty member is being considered for promotion and tenure.

The matter of the rank and tenure of committee members can come to play when serious differences among them occur. The veteran advisor with high rank, tenure, and considerable experience in working with dissertation committees will usually avoid difficult situations by advising you, the doctoral student, as to who should and should not be on your committee. It is also our view that the whole dissertation committee system depends to a large extent on committee members showing some, if not a lot, of deference to the committee chair. Part of this deference exists because junior faculty members need the approval of senior faculty members in order to be recommended for tenure and/or improvement in rank. This is simply a reality with regard to power relationships in universities. [It should be noted that final formal approval for promotions and tenure reside with the head of the university or university system with all bodies below this status serving as recommending bodies.]

If you have the kind of relationship with your dissertation advisor that lends itself to candid conversations, these issues may be brought to your attention *by your advisor*. Our advice is for you to be aware of such issues without bringing undue attention to them. Keep in mind that "loose lips sink ships," an expression from world wars in the last century. Most persons with whom you talk will tell at least one person what you said. We asked a senior colleague at her retirement party what advice she would give doctoral students and beginning faculty members. She replied, "Just tell them I've never been sorry for anything I *didn't* say."

Your Fellow Doctoral Students

Some doctoral students who began as acquaintances will become colleagues during the dissertation stage. In this new role they will serve as important sources of guidance. You will quickly come to appreciate and respect the academic abilities of some of your fellow students as you move forward with your dissertation. Conversations with them in formal and informal settings will introduce you to topics and literature related to your own research and writing interests. Fellow students may also help you with Internet searches, organizing references with the most recent software packages, data-gathering, and assessing research methods appropriate for your dissertation topic. They may even participate in the gathering of data for you.

Doctoral students have shared with us their appreciation for fellow students who have assisted in suggesting styles of tabular and graphic displays. One small group of students used lunches together to explore such displays so that it became a kind of fun game that led to fine academic work. (See appendix F, "Working Alone and Working As a Team Member.")

Technical support is often complemented by inspirational and emotional support from fellow dissertation students who will help you stay on track. In the words of one doctoral graduate, "It is important to remember as a doctoral student that you and other doctoral students share one goal. You want to get out of there with degree in hand." Dissertation research and writing may become lonely activities unless you and your fellow students make the effort to stay in touch with each other on a sustained basis. Several doctoral students who worked with us sorted themselves off as pairs that met each Saturday in the library. Each person's responsibility to the other kept them on track.

It is important to acknowledge that competition among doctoral students is a reality. A student who was positioning herself for success after graduation by being outspoken in taking on other students in classes and at the dissertation stage found herself isolated by peers. She didn't understand the coolness toward her by other students. Another doctoral graduate gave the following advice: "Occasionally a professor will 'flip out' about something or other and students will say to each other 'I don't want to turn into that.' At the time it seemed both funny and serious and we had to warn ourselves not to talk too much about the incident as faculty have a lot of power, and it can get you into a lot of trouble if you appear to be indiscreet and mean."

Professors and Other Experts Outside of Your Department

We have noted in our work with students at the dissertation stage that it is easy to stay within the comfort and security of their own dissertation committees, thereby overlooking important sources of guidance outside of this committee and the department in which they are getting their degree. One student shared the following with us upon recognizing this reality. "I am reluctant to approach a professor in our university who has done considerable research and writing on a topic related to my dissertation because she is not on my dissertation committee. I don't want to take time away from her other activities, and I feel somewhat guilty for not asking her to be on my committee, but my dissertation advisor and I didn't think it would be a good fit."

We responded by saying that there are a number of ways to connect with this professor that will enhance your dissertation even though she isn't on your committee. For example, she frequently gives speeches and serves on panel discussions that you can attend. And, if you wish to follow up on these experiences you can schedule an individual conference with her. We added that professors are flattered when students demonstrate interest in their research and writing, and they may be relieved at times not to serve on dissertation committees due to heavy involvement in other activities. You can recognize these realities without discussing them with these professors.

Dissertation students who adopt a proactive stance often profit from contacts with professors and experts in other institutions. You can contact these persons by phone, fax, e-mail, or regular mail. The e-mails of professional organization members are increasingly available and using Google can often yield contact information of value. Research and writings of experts can also be received in this manner. State as specifically as possible what you wish to know when you get in touch with these people. Be sure to save hard copy, electronic copy, and notes you have taken *in the words of experts* so that when you cite what they say it has the air of authenticity. (See appendix P, "Note Taking as an Important Part of the Research and Writing Process.") You will need their permission to quote them in your dissertation. Your dissertation chair and committee members will respect your going the extra mile to get this information.

Drawing on Your Own Experiences

As a doctoral student you have been conditioned by your formal education to locate authority outside of yourself rather than in your own experiences. Textbooks, lectures, and assigned readings are considered the fount of knowledge. We urge our doctoral students to write down, often in outline form, everything they know and feel about a dissertation topic *before* engaging in dissertation research and writing. In this way you won't discount your original ideas and feelings.

You may well question and change your mind about the ideas and feelings you have before doing the dissertation but such views and predispositions can serve you well as a benchmark in your dissertation journey. They will be a starting place or springboard that can lead to a more comprehensive critique of matters you are researching. (See appendix C, "The Power of Critique.") It almost goes without saying that your own attitude toward what you have experienced shouldn't lead to a narcissism that compounds your ignorance. It is sometimes difficult to let go of ideas that you thought were so precious.

There is another way that you can log your ideas and feelings as you write your dissertation. We suggest that you write down and date each dissertation title and subtitle that you adopt. Our students find this an interesting record of changes in direction that their dissertation takes. The following serves as an example:

September 10, 2011	The Integration of Goffman's Presentation of Self Model and Sarason's Creation of Settings Model for Special Education Students
October 30, 2011	The Merger of Two Social Science Frameworks for Reaching Special Education Students
December 1, 2011	The Presentation of Self and the Creation of Settings for Special Education Students: A Case Study Approach
February 7, 2012	The Presentation of Self and the Creation of Settings for Special Education Students: A Case Study Approach in an Urban Setting
June 10, 2012	The Creation of a Leadership Framework for Reaching Special Education Students: A Case Study Approach in a Detroit High School

With the help of dissertation committee members, the doctoral student selected a title that readers were likely to find interesting and a subtitle that would locate the study in a particular high school and city. (See appendix M, "Giving Your Dissertation a Title and Subtitle in Relation to the Definitions Section of the Dissertation.") The key words or indicators in the title and subtitle will bring important attention to your research and writing and be of immense value to veteran researchers, students at the dissertation stage and students considering dissertation topics.

Valuing your own experiences can be very helpful in keeping the momentum as you do dissertation research and writing. At first glance, you may think that you have to work your way through the dissertation from the first chapter to the last in linear fashion. This perfectionistic tendency can get you stuck in one of the stages.

By valuing your own experiences, you can do some hopping back and forth among the stages to keep your momentum. A doctoral student describes this matter: "I must have written chapter one twenty times. At first I thought it had to be perfectly etched in stone so that I could move on to other chapters. I realized with time that in writing others chapters I could return to chapter one and rewrite it with enriched meaning and insight. The same kind of thing happened with chapter two on related literature. I discovered new sources to cite as I moved to other chapters. My dissertation advisor taught me that a creative dissertation is sometimes more of a collage than a textbook. He had a plaque above his desk in his university office with a quote from his mentor, Seymour Sarason, Professor Emeritus of Psychology at Yale University:

"ALMOST EVERYTHING I HAVE EVER DONE OR WRITTEN HAS BEEN AUTOBIOGRAPHICAL" (Seymour B. Sarason, 1988, p. 231).

Professional Literature

The literature refers to books, academic journals and conference proceedings that are related to the dissertation topic you have chosen. Unpublished theses and dissertations will also provide you with sources of guidance for your research and writing. It is important that you state clearly the key roles of your literature review to avoid treating this task as a dumping ground for miscellaneous and often irrelevant information. Each cited source should have a *direct application* to your study and therefore help

- (a) locate your study among similar published studies, (b) identify strengths and limitations of those studies, and (c) demonstrate what contribution your study can make to that domain of knowledge,
- (a) show what methods have been used in the past to investigate your kind of research problem, (b) identify strengths and limitations of those methods, and (c) explain why the method you are using is appropriate for your case, and/or
- in the analysis and interpretation of your findings, show how your results agree with and/or differ from the findings and interpretations of relevant studies in the professional literature (Thomas & Brubaker, 2001, p. 24).

The Internet has overtaken in-print library holdings as a source of information that will be useful to you for your literature search. Key words in your dissertation title and perhaps subtitle will generate a list of websites related to such words. Material can be easily copied in entirety or selected passages, after which it can be pasted into a Word-processing file. You have discovered by now in your doctoral program how important it is to accurately record the source of material taken from periodicals, books and websites (author's name, title of the source, date, publisher, page numbers). Students share with us horror stories of trying to chase down such information when it is not initially recorded. This problem can slow down your research and writing and annoy you to no end.

It is important to note that the process of publishing scholarly articles and books contains a quality-assessment component often missing from websites. Experts in the field in which academic publishing takes place are asked to judge manuscripts submitted. You, your advisor, and your dissertation committee will need to judge the quality of research and writing you wish to cite. Consistency across websites, author qualifications, and author perspectives will be considerations as to trustworthiness. This paragraph on quality assessment may be one that you wish to cite in your dissertation when you describe how you have dealt with the matter of trustworthiness.

There is a source of literature review often overlooked by dissertation students. First-rate book reviewers describe far more than chapter contents. They often bring their rich experience as reviewers, researchers, and authors to their critiques of important books. Their fresh insights and perspectives may be very helpful to you as you assess books that speak to your dissertation research and writing. Reviews may be found in periodicals and on the Internet. Barnes and Noble (www.bn.com) and Amazon (www.amazon.com) furnish reviews on their list. *Book Review Digest*, a monthly publication that's issued also in an annual cumulative volume and *Book Review Index*, a bimonthly periodical that helps you get to particular books, are useful sources of book reviews. The journal *Choice* offers analyses of books for college and university libraries.

CHOOSING RESEARCH TOPICS

"The two things you need to know as you hunt for a dissertation topic are (a) what to look for and (b) where to look" (Thomas & Brubaker, 2001, p. 5). There are several general types of research topics:

- Ready-made topics, such as those connected with research being conducted by your dissertation advisor or a member of your dissertation committee, the advantage being that you can serve as a research assistant, the disadvantage being that the job can be very intense and demanding.
- Risky topics that may lead to negative results considered to be of little or no value and not being able to get the information needed to answer your research question.

- Pursuing a personal mission, such as helping at-risk students and adults, the advantage being that you will have a passion for doing the research, the disadvantage being that you may get lost in the subjectivity of your passion (Thomas & Brubaker, 2001, pp. 9–15).

How then can you, the dissertation student, judge the suitability of a dissertation topic? Three questions will help you provide an answer to this question. First, is the topic appropriate to your major field of study? Second, will the results of the study make a contribution to knowledge? Third, is the study feasible?

Sources and Kinds of Research Problems

Now that you are at the dissertation stage, it is important that you constantly be on the alert for research problems worthy of investigating. There is no substitute for critical reading and listening as you move forward. Furthermore, you must be alert to problems you encounter on your own job or hear about from others concerning their work. Doctoral students sometimes pick up research problems and related research and writing in attending conference sessions. Some of these sessions focus on dissertation research and writing.

Critical Reading and Listening

Questions and inquiries you have while reading and listening can concern (a) the significance or focus of an author's research topic, (b) the applicability of an author's results to other populations, times, or places, (c) a researcher's methods of collecting information, (d) ways data have been classified, (e) an author's theory (map of the territory) of what causes events to occur as they do, (f) applications of theories, or (g) some combination of several of these matters (Thomas & Brubaker, 2008, pp. 56–57).

If you are interested in applicability in general and replication possibilities in particular, two questions will guide you: "Would the same conclusions result from studying a different sample of people, institutions, events, or time periods? What kind of sample might yield different results, and why?"

Because there are different methods of collecting information, you will want to consider seeking answers to a question someone else has studied by employing a different method of gathering data. As a result, the innovative contribution you will make in your dissertation is threefold. You will (a) introduce the academic community to your data collection technique, along with a description of its strengths and limitations, (b) show how the results obtained with your procedure compare with the results reported in what you have read, and (c) offer your estimate of why the outcomes of the two studies were similar and/or different (Thomas & Brubaker, 2008, p. 58).

Problems Encountered on the Job

Your success at work largely depends on your ability to address problems. Prior to beginning work on your dissertation, you probably had a very pragmatic stance in relation to these problems. That is, you critiqued the problem, considered possible solutions and then took steps to deal with the problem in the most efficient way possible. (See appendix C, "The Power of Critique.") Now that you have a critical and discerning eye out for possible research problems to be addressed in your dissertation, you will want to use the critical thinking, research, and writing skills you have learned in your doctoral program. The fact that you have experienced the problem(s) on the job will bring a degree of authenticity to your dissertation research and writing that will have the ring of truth. This is something that your dissertation advisor, dissertation committee members, and other readers of your dissertation will like and respect. You will communicate that you know the game and the score.

How to Distinguish a Good Topic from a Bad One

Nine criteria or standards for judging the desirability of research problems can be helpful to you in choosing a dissertation topic (Thomas & Brubaker, 2008, pp. 65–68).

Committee Approval

Do the members of your dissertation committee approve of your proposed research problem? You will know that such approval is granted when your committee signs off on your dissertation proposal. You will have successfully provided a rationale telling why the problem is a good one and what methods you plan to use for gathering and analyzing your data. If any of your committee members consider your proposal unacceptable, you will either have to change your problem or replace dissenting committee members with ones who approve of your topic. You will need to work with your advisor on this issue.

Remember that the signatures by committee members on your dissertation proposal constitute your contract with the university. Students sometimes fail to remember this and panic if problems concerning the proposal arise. When such problems do occur, you and your dissertation committee chair can review the dissertation proposal and remind committee members of this document if your advisor feels this needs to be done. If necessary, your advisor may have to take this matter to higher levels of the administration.

True Research

Committee members often differ in what they consider to be true research. You will realize this in attending conferences and conventions where research is discussed, and this will also be clear to you as professors are engaged in informal conversations on campus about what research really matters. These are serious matters to professors as promotion and tenure decisions as well as merit pay judgments regarding their own research and writing have or will be made that affect their careers and lives. Strong ego involvement is the order of the day. Therefore, it is important that your definition of research coincides with that of the professors who supervise and assess your work. An honest discussion of such matters is essential so that you and your committee members get straight signals from each other.

Outcome Significance

Will the outcomes of your research be considered significant by the readers for whom your dissertation is intended? The complexity and level of expertise of your research and writing expected by committee members must be up to their standards. You will therefore be expected to indicate for whom—and why—an answer to your research question is important. You may wish to review other dissertations, including those of your dissertation committee members to see how they addressed this issue. Your dissertation advisor may be especially helpful regarding this matter.

Feasible Methodology

Does your research problem appear solvable with the methods of investigation you have in mind? It will be up to you to describe your research question in a manner that convinces your committee that the methodology you plan to use will produce credible results. Sharing with your committee how you arrived at this research problem is often useful and convincing to committee members. Your dissertation advisor can be most helpful in advising you on this issue.

Time Constraint

Can the dissertation research and writing be completed within the available time period? Time constraints imposed by (a) the college or university (some schools set a limit of seven years for completing a doctorate) and (b) other time consuming responsibilities in students' lives (a job, a family) are an important consideration. It is wise for you to present a time table to your committee with each phase of the dissertation highlighted. They will understand that this table is proximate and subject to revision. We have been surprised by the number of doctoral students who are not knowledgeable about university regulations with regard to the number of years in which they must complete the doctorate and policies with regard to extensions. Anxiety invoked when they find out can induce tremendous stress.

Required Knowledge and Skills

Do you already have the knowledge and skills required for completing your dissertation research and writing? If not, how and when do you intend to acquire them? This often becomes an important issue with regard to research design and competencies. Students are nervous as to their degree of expertise concerning research methodology(ies). They then have to convince their dissertation committee members that they have access to experts who will help them to a reasonable degree. There are obviously specialized skills that are required with regard to computer programming and the like, and students must be honest enough to know what they don't know and how to get the knowledge they need. Your candor on these matters will be appreciated by committee members.

Students sometimes experience difficulty with regard to the kind and amount of help they receive from research methodology experts. It is essential that you are able to understand and articulate the help you have received at the dissertation defense. It is not enough to simply cite the work of an expert who has helped you. It is important that you work with your dissertation advisor if you anticipate any problems in this matter. Keeping a log on contacts you made with a research expert can be helpful in reconstructing the kind and degree of help you received.

Equipment and Supplies

What facilities will you need to carry out your dissertation research and writing, and how do you intend to acquire them? Committee members may ask for details in answer to this question. Some research activities may demand more resources than others and you should be prepared to make adjustments in your estimates.

Personnel

Who will perform each of the jobs required for carrying out your dissertation research and writing? Sometimes students will be the sole participants but other dissertation research required outside help—people who serve as interviewers, test correctors, statistical analysts, and more. There is no substitute for a good copy editor, *a person who can make significant changes in your manuscript writing,* and proofreaders, those who make simple grammatical and spelling corrections and the like.

You should not assume that any English major will be a good copy editor. You must be in sync with the person who plays this role. Talking to doctoral graduates about who they used as copy editors and the quality of their work is essential. If you can see the kinds of corrections a copy editor has made on another person's manuscript, this can be of immeasurable value as you decide who hire to do this important work. Many students have been delayed for some time by the work of poor copy editors. A good deal of money can be wasted on inadequate copy editors and proofreaders.

Funds

What expenses do you expect to incur, and how do you expect to pay them? Your dissertation advisor and committee members may ask how much your project is expected to cost and where the money will come from. You should be prepared to present a total amount and detailed breakdown of expenses. The source of such funds should also be identified. Ask recent doctoral graduates who have used research methodologies similar to the one(s) you wish to use what expected and unexpected costs they incurred. One student was shocked, for instance by the costs of postage and transportation.

STATING THE RESEARCH PROBLEM AND ITS RATIONALE

Dissertation students often make the mistake of beating around the bush without clearly stating the research problem and its rationale. A surprising number of our students have had to deal with this problem more than once. We suggest that you begin this section of the dissertation with introductory sentences like "The research problem is . . ." and "The rationale for the research problem is . . ."

Differences among dissertation committee members will naturally arise, but most members will at least want a clear statement of your research problem, your reasons for choosing it, and a concise description of how you hope to find a solution "Two popular ways to state a research problem are as a question and as a hypothesis" (Thomas & Brubaker, 2008, p. 86). *The distinction between a question and a hypothesis is one of the most important but neglected issues our doctoral students have encountered.* By casting a research problem in the form of a question, you will suggest the kind of answer being sought, with that suggestion then guiding decisions about the investigation methods you will employ.

A hypothesis represents a probable answer to the research question, but the probability that the answer is corrected still needs to be tested through more investigation. This leads us to the matter of which of these approaches is preferable—a question or a hypothesis? And, in what circumstances is one better than the other? The hypothesis is better than the question when two conditions exist. One, when there is good reason to believe that a proposed solution to the research issue is correct, but that belief still needs to be corroborated or refuted by evidence. The other is when you plan to apply a statistical test to the data you collect, and casting the problem as a hypothesis renders statistical testing more convenient.

However, most problems can be expressed as questions that involve who, how, which, why what, when, where, how much, how frequently, or several of these. It should be added that often a topic is best expressed as two or more questions, sometimes with minor questions subsumed under major ones. Sorting this out is one of the most important decisions you will make.

Two important purposes are served by your being obliged to state your topic precisely and concisely. First, the statement guides you in charting the steps to take toward solving the problem. Second, it makes clear to your dissertation advisor and committee members what you intend to do, thus expediting their task of evaluating your proposal and offering advice (see Thomas & Brubaker, 2008, pp. 86–89).

In conclusion, when you submit your research proposal to your dissertation committee, you will be expected to furnish a written synopsis that defines the research problem or issue, suggest why it's important to investigate, and explain the research methods you intend to use for resolving the problem or question. It is wise for you to get reactions to your research proposal from one or more trusted persons along with your dissertation advisor.

DEFINING KEY TERMS

We have witnessed many dissertation defenses in which dissertation students simply don't define key terms. For example, one student defined "curriculum" as what one learns from life experiences. Most committee members defined "curriculum" as the course of study. The student ended up with a separate definitions section in Chapter One that defined "predetermined curriculum" as the course of study and "emerging curriculum" as what happens and what is learned in reacting to the predetermined curriculum and unexpected life experiences. The student was challenged to go through the entire dissertation making sure that the terms defined in Chapter One were used in a way that was consistent with these definitions.

This simply makes the point that different people bring different meanings to the words they use in speaking and writing. You won't be able to move forward with your dissertation research and writing unless you and your committee members agree on key terms.

Among the most basic terms are those found in a dissertation's title or topic question. These terms will serve as a kind of map for persons interested in your dissertation and those who read the dissertation for their own purposes. They will see by terms defined how you framed your dissertation.

There are four ways that you can define key terms: (a) providing synonyms, (b) furnishing sentence descriptions, (c) citing shared experience or knowledge, and (d) defining by the operations used in conducting the research.

Synonyms

Synonyms rarely suffice as they too frequently carry as many different meanings—often vague meanings—as the words they are supposed to elucidate. For the most part, the only occasions on which synonyms are suitable are ones in which a new, unfamiliar word can be clarified with a familiar word or phrase. This can occur with places (Queen City in North Carolina = Charlotte, North Carolina), people (Muhammad Ali = Cassius Clay), institutions or agencies (State Department = foreign relations department), or conditions (flu = influenza).

Sentence Descriptions

A single sentence, or a few sentences, may be adequate to explain the meaning a dissertation student assigns to a term within the boundaries of the dissertation. The word "education" will refer to formal education in K–12 classrooms. It may be helpful to add what a key word is not intended to include. This is to rule out unintended meaning that readers might reasonably assume unless they are told otherwise.

Shared Experiences

Sentence definitions can be usefully enhanced with lifelike examples that serve as clarifying experiences shared by you and your readers. The word "setting" refers to any instance where two or more people with common goals

get together for a sustained period of time. (See Sarason, 1972, p. 1.) Friend-
ships, marriages, and small groups serve as examples.

Operational Definitions

Defining a key term operationally consists of specifying the techniques used
for measuring or assessing the characteristic that the term signifies. In this
dissertation, *academic aptitude* is defined by the scores students earn on
the Educational Testing Service's computerized version of the *Scholastic
Aptitude Test*, edition 2010.

In conclusion, it is not necessary to limit yourself to only one of the several
ways of defining terms. You may often find it best to cast one definition as a
sentence, another as several sentences elaborate with lifelike examples, and a
third as the procedures used for measuring the variable that is being defined.
The methods you choose can depend on which type you believe will be most
precisely understood by readers, and which type guides you most accurately
in selecting data-gathering techniques and interpreting the data. (See Thomas
& Brubaker, 2008, pp. 89–93).

In the event that you wish to do more with the important matter of definitions, we recommend a classic work, the best one of its kind: Israel Scheffler's
The Language of Education (Springfield, Illinois: Charles C. Thomas, originally published in 1960). Professor Scheffler was a professor of education
and philosophy at Harvard University when he wrote this seminal work. Your
using and referencing this book, particularly if questions are raised on your
treatment of definitions, will impress your dissertation committee.

In Chapter 1, Scheffler refers to three kinds of definitions: (1) *descriptive
definitions* that describe conventional ways in which a term has been used;
(2) *stipulative definitions* describe the special sense in which a term is used;
and (3) *programmatic definitions* that refer to the way a term is used in a
practical program on a particular occasion. (See Scheffler, 1960, pp. 11–35.)
The following demonstrates how Scheffler's definitions may be used in a
dissertation:

- *Curriculum*: the course of study or body of knowledge that is expected to
  be learned by students, primarily in schools and institutions of higher edu-
  cation (a descriptive definition).
- *Inner Curriculum*: what each person experiences as learning settings are
  cooperatively created (Brubaker, 2004, p. 22) (a stipulative definition).
- *University of North Carolina at Greensboro's Humanistic Education
  Curriculum*: a program designed to promote citizenship education (Zahorik
  & Brubaker, 1972, p. 3) (a programmatic definition).

How can you use Scheffler's work in your dissertation? We advise you to begin by introducing his framework with its three kinds of definitions and then follow by identifying and defining key terms used in your research and writing, terms often found in your dissertation's title and subtitle. After each term with its definition you can cite one or more of the three kinds of definitions in the Scheffler framework, much as it is done in the preceding paragraph.

PROVIDING A RATIONALE

A rationale consists of a line of reasoning that (a) describes a context within which to locate the intended dissertation research and writing and (b) justifying the methods you plan to use for solving your research problem.

The rationale plays a role at two stages of your dissertation process: (a) when you submit your research proposal to your committee members for their advice and approval and (b) when you write your final version of the dissertation so readers will understand the contribution to practice that your dissertation represents (Thomas & Brubaker, 2008, pp. 93–96).

Placing Your Work in Context

Locating your work in a context consists of identifying a domain of life into which the dissertation research fits. A popular way to do this is to introduce a label that you assume is familiar to your readers. A hypothetical study of Mexican American families uses labels that descend from the general to the specific. The first label—*social change*—places your work within a very broad field. The second—*family structure*—identifies a more limited realm. The third—*trends in family structure and function among Mexican Americans*—represents a very narrow field, indeed. Your rationale might start with the label that signifies the field in which you think your work belongs.

> Among theories of social change, the most prominent types . . .
> The literature on family structure can be divided into . . .
> Investigations of trends in family structure and function among Mexican
>   Americans treat such issues as . . .

Your next task is that of showing how your project fits into the selected realm. Here is one way that could be done for the second option—family structure.

The literature on family structure can be divided into six categories focusing on (1) family members' roles, (2) types of human needs met within different family structures, (3) nuclear and extended forms of family, (4) lineage and governance (e.g., patrilineal, matrilineal), (5) explanations of family structural change over time, and (6) cross-cultural comparisons. The present study links the second and fifth of these categories by addressing the question, What changes have occurred in the structure and functions of Mexican American families during the twentieth century, and what trends do such changes reflect? In addition, by centering attention on a particular ethnic group—Mexican Americans—the study provides materials useful to people interested in the last of the categories, that of cross-cultural comparisons.

Identifying Your Intended Contribution

The most important function of your rationale may be the explanation of how the dissertation can contribute to knowledge (*basic research* that corrects or expands people's understanding of the world) and/or to practice (*applied research* that improves the conduct of some aspect of life). This function is accomplished by your identifying shortcoming in the existing body of knowledge or practice that could be remedied by the proposed research.

Describing Your Data Collection Methods

You may wish to submit your proposal in two stages. The first stage consists of describing your research question and supporting that choice with a rationale. This will give you a sense of your advisor's opinion about the suitability of your topic before you go to the trouble of working out a data-gathering plan. If your topic and its rationale are judged to be acceptable—either in their original state or in a revised version—you move ahead to specifying your methodology.

RESEARCH DESIGN

Constructing a research design is one of the most challenging steps in the dissertation writing process. Your dissertation research design will demonstrate how the various parts of the research project relate to each other so that you can address the major research questions. You will probably write about your research design in a general way in Chapter One, *Introduction*, with a more specific description in Chapter Three, commonly titled *Methodology*.

Collecting information, organizing information, summarizing information, and interpreting information are processes common to all dissertations. Collecting information can consists of five phases:

(a) identifying the kinds of information needed to answer the research questions

(b) identifying potential sources of that information (books, journals, public documents, people to question or test, kinds of experiments to conduct)
(c) choosing among the sources
(d) devising efficient methods and instruments for gathering the information
(e) compiling the desired data by means of those methods and instruments

General research methods may include the following:

- historical accounts (descriptive chronicles, interpretive histories, biographies and autobiographies);
- case studies and ethnographies;
- experience narratives;
- surveys;
- correlation analyses; and
- experiments (Thomas & Brubaker, 2008, pp. 99–148).

Choosing a suitable design can entail three principal steps: (1) considering the characteristics of different experimental designs, (2) deciding whether one of those designs will be the most appropriate method for answering your research question (or will some other approach—historical, case-study, survey—be more relevant?), and (3) choosing a design that will furnish the most convincing evidence about the problem you are investigating within your research context (Thomas & Brubaker, 2008, p. 148).

There are five procedures and instruments useful for collecting data in research projects: observations, content analyses, interviews, questionnaires, and tests (Thomas & Brubaker, 2008, pp. 154–184).

Specific information related to this general introduction to research design may be found in R. Murray Thomas & Dale L. Brubaker, 2008, *Theses and Dissertations: A Guide to Planning, Research, and Writing* (Corwin Press: Thousand Oaks, CA).

In the interest of introducing you to the construction of a dissertation research design, we now take you backstage into the life of a doctoral student by presenting a snapshot of his proactive decision making.

Snapshot 6.2

Resourcing Your Methodology

I had always heard that good leaders surround themselves with those who can make up for their weaknesses. This was a lesson I found quite helpful as I envisioned the type of dissertation research I would conduct. I found this principle to be especially important in my statistical design and analysis. Even though I consider myself to be math-oriented, and I worked hard to understand the various methodologies in my statistics courses, I still felt quite overwhelmed when trying to apply this information to my dissertation. I had always heard that you could pay someone to help with the statistical analysis, but I was too cheap (and poor) and do this. My solution was to get to know a professor in the educational measurement program.

I can still remember sitting outside of Dr. Miller's office, working in the lab space, and reviewing my work with him periodically to make sure I was using the statistical software correctly. It was amazing how much I had forgotten from his classes, and even after reviewing my class notes, I realized that I needed his help. As Dr. Miller also shared an interest in my content area, homelessness, he was an ideal fit to be on my dissertation committee. Not everyone had this kind of support on their committee, but we were all fortunate in that the faculty in this program were always open to providing their help.

Additionally, as I considered implementing my research study, I decided to solicit the help of a couple of master's students I had gotten to know in my program. A professor agreed to provide independent study course credit if I supervised them, which I was glad to do. This gave me a chance to mentor them while gaining two research partners who would help me collect data and process these experiences. In fact, both students became official co-investigators on the Institutional Review Board (IRB) proposal and shared in the experience of learning how to design, implement, and report on a research study. The three of us wrote an article together on the experience, and now one is applying for doctoral studies on her own. What joy it gave me to write her a letter of recommendation! What began as a search for additional resources to complete a large data gathering project became a chance to mentor two outstanding students, the same type of work that I would continue as an assistant professor in my first faculty job.

DEVELOPING A DISSERTATION PROPOSAL

It is customary for universities to require doctoral candidates to submit a written description of their intended research project to the faculty members who will supervise their dissertation work. (See appendix L, "Example of a Traditional Table of Contents for a Dissertation.") In many universities a student's dissertation officially begins with the acceptance of the candidate's proposal. The proposal—sometimes called a *prospectus* or *plan*—is a statement of the problem on which the dissertation will focus. The proposal is presented to all members of the dissertation committee after the student's advisor feels it is ready for scrutiny.

There is no one form in which proposals are prepared. The form you adopt can depend on several things—the university's or department's regulations, your advisor's preference, the stage of your progress on your research problem, the complexity of your topic, your own preference—any of these. There are certain elements common to most dissertation proposals. They usually begin with a description of your topic and why you chose it followed by a discussion of your intended research methods, such as what sort of evidence you'll collect, whatever theory—if any—you'll use, and how you'll compile or organize the evidence. Proposals vary as to the detail presented. (See Thomas & Brubaker, 2001, pp. 39–43.)

Many departments with doctoral programs offer dissertation proposal seminars. The following snapshot will give you a sense of what might take place in such a seminar.

Snapshot 6.3

A Notable Dissertation Proposal Seminar

Professor Lee is known as a dissertation advisor whose students finish their degrees. Although he was not my advisor, I knew that getting into his dissertation proposal seminar would be helpful. I therefore signed up for it and joined ten other students during the fall semester.

We struggled as a class to get a handle on writing the prospectus as Professor Lee gave us a number of tips that were useful:

- It is important to recognize your audience. Your immediate audience is your advisor and dissertation committee. Without their signatures, you simply won't get your doctorate. Your secondary audience is anyone who becomes interested in the subject of your work—something that is usually the result of their seeing the title of your dissertation. Your challenge is to fashion a title and perhaps subtitle that will give the reader clear and sufficient information about your research and writing. The title is frequently somewhat general whereas the subtitle is usually more specific, perhaps locating where your study took place, the research methodology you chose and persons influenced by the research. For example, ONE SCHOOL OR TWO? A Case Study of a Large Public High School in North Carolina.

- The contextual problem in the larger society or an institution in society, such as public schools, is connected to, but not the same thing as, the research problem. "Two popular ways to stage a research problem are as a question and as a hypothesis" (Thomas & Brubaker, 2000, p. 77). This quote or a paraphrase of it is a good way to introduce the section of your dissertation proposal in which you spell out your question and/ or hypotheses. It demonstrates that you know your way around the research "orchard."
- Italicize the terms you define in order to make them stand out—get the attention of the reader.
- In your methodology section of the proposal outline, define the methodology(ies) you will use and cite the advantages of using such methodology(ies).
- Try to limit your headings in the review of literature chapter to three or four. Each heading is simply a two to four word theme or subject.
- Triangulation of evidence speaks to *the validity question.* You will need to define triangulation in this part of your proposal.

It was interesting to observe how these specific suggestions and discussions in class helped each of us begin to put together pieces of the puzzle called a dissertation proposal. Everything seemed to come together during one of the three-hour classes near the end of the semester. Professor Lee was asked by one of the students how personal a proposal and dissertation should be. Professor Lee responded, *"The dissertation doesn't have to be a personal testimony, but it should have personal meaning."*

At the end of the class, Professor Lee asked each student to add to a "verbal collage" on the personal meaning each student had acquired during the seminar. They responded as follows:

- "This class helped me organize the research and writing process and gave me permission to be passionate about my work." Bonnie
- "I've avoided hell and now have a template for reflection and action." Denise
- "A mystery has been revealed." Billy
- "This process prompted me to have a special meeting with my advisor that I would not have had before." Rita
- "I now have focus and have learned the importance of clearly defining what I want to do." Lynette
- "I don't cope well 'learning on the fly.' I now have the big picture." Steve

- "I was in undiscovered country. Before it was a mysterious nature and I wasn't sure what I wanted to do. I now have a map." David
- "I now have focus. I have insight into process and have set priorities. I can now entertain ambiguity." Tosha
- "I now understand how important it is to be passionate about what I'm doing. I can do it! I'm amazed at how others like my topic—a real incentive for me." Toni
- "Being engaged in this process brought discipline to me. I learned to bring precision to my work—such as defining terms clearly. I learned to frame a question and situate it in the literature." Martha
- "This was an opportunity to find out more about myself—a way to share what's inside of me." Mel

In conclusion, I learned from a community of fellow doctoral students, under the fine leadership of Professor Lee, the value of colleagueship and individual scholarship. The balance between teamwork and individual work is the secret to successfully completing the doctorate. (See appendix F, "Working Alone and Working As a Team Member.)

The following outline of a dissertation proposal will give you an idea of some of the key elements that may be included.

Title: *The Effects of Financial Stress in Higher Education*
Author: Robin Ganzert, University of North Carolina at Greensboro. (See Thomas & Brubaker, 2008, pp. 325–329.)

1. Introduction
   The financial function of an institution of higher education serves as a vital factor in the institution's long-term viability and success. The issue of financial stress in higher education is important for administrators to address, preferably in a proactive stance prior to crisis rather than as a reaction to a specific financial crisis. The importance and timeliness of this subject is apparent in reading almost any issue of the *Chronicle of Higher Education.*

2. Statement of the Problem
   The problem that will be addressed in this study is the determination of the patterns and processes used to address financial crisis in institutions of higher education. The study will explore the sources of financial stress, and the responses to financial stress during times of financial crisis.

3. Definition of Key Terms
    3.1 Financial stress is defined as an influence which disrupts or distresses the financial function in the institution's operations.
    3.2 Environmental scanning is defined as the identification of environmental factors and the importance of those factors to the institution.

4. Research Questions
    4.1 What are the major sources of current financial stress in institutions of education today?
    4.2 What are the responses of the institutions to financial stress?
    4.3 How are the core functions (academic, marketing, and admissions) affected by financial stress?
    4.4 Where are the financial stresses evident (e.g., the endowment funds, operating funds, or the plant funds)?
    4.5 How is the response to the financial stress reflected in the annual budgeting parameters or guidelines?
    4.6 What is the institutional strategic planning response to financial stress in higher education?
    4.7 What are the patterns of information flow used to solve financial crisis situations?
    4.8 What are the roles of the president, chief academic officer, and chief financial officer in times of financial crisis at institutions?
    4.9 How do the decision-making processes regarding financial crisis affect the culture of the institution?

5. Study Methodology (Two Related Methods)
    5.1 Multiple case studies
        5.1.1 Five university sites
        5.1.2 Interviews of presidents, CAOs, and CFOs
        5.1.3 Focus on contemporary events, no control over behavioral events by researcher
    5.2 Descriptive study
        5.2.1 Survey driven by case interviews
        5.2.2 Stratified business officers
        5.2.3 Piloted with regional senior finance experts

6. Review of Related Literature (Key Indicators or Headings)
    6.1 Sources of financial stress
    6.2 Trends in response to financial stress
    6.3 Proactive strategies for response to financial stress
    6.4 The statesman role and the fiscal administrator
    6.5 An historical examination of financial stress in higher education

6.6 Timeline of financial stress in higher education

6.7 Implications of financial stress in higher education

6.8 The financial stressors in the modern curriculum

7. Tests of Research Design (Tests, Case Study Tactics, and Phases of Research in Which Tactic Occurs) See power point presentation.

8. Triangulation of Evidence
   8.1 Public documents/reports (newspapers, financial statements)
   8.2 Internal documents
   8.3 Administrator interviews

9. Case Study Protocol
   9.1 Opening interview question: "What are your experiences with financial stress at your institution?"
   9.2 Possible follow-up research questions:
   "What is the major source of financial stress at your institution?
   "How did your institution respond to the financial stress?"
   "Where are the financial stresses evident at your institution (e.g., what fund)?"
   "How is your institution's response to financial stress reflected in the annual budgeting parameters?"
   "What is the strategic planning response to financial stress on your campus?"
   "How does information flow during times of financial stress?"
   "Any additional comments?"
   9.3 Pilot case study at selected institution

10. Survey
    10.1 Survey questions developed in interviews
    10.2 Piloted by a panel of experts
    10.3 Stratified sample of chief financial officers

11. Conclusion (study's contribution)
    11.1 The study will provide insights into the organizational decision-making processes in times of significant financial stress.
    11.2 The study will provide insights into the planning for and response to financial stress, and the impact upon institutions of higher education. (See Thomas & Brubaker, 2008, pp. 325–329.)

In conclusion, the dissertation proposal can be a valuable map that gets you on the road to researching and writing an excellent dissertation. It should be viewed as a springboard that gives you the security of working with a plan while at the same time entertaining changes that naturally evolve in creative research and writing. We should add that some dissertation research proposals can be turned into the first three chapters of the dissertation with certain revisions.

GETTING APPROVAL FROM THE INSTITUTIONAL REVIEW BOARD

Universities with doctoral programs have offices and/or committees to advance and monitor research, teaching, and other creative efforts. Offices may have titles like the Office of Research Compliance. It is at the dissertation proposal stage of your doctoral program that you will probably become acquainted with the Institutional Review Board (IRB) or a similar body such as the Ethical Review Board (ERB) or the Independent Ethics Committee (IEC). It is the responsibility of such bodies to protect the rights and welfare of research subjects.

Critical approval and oversight of research conducted on human subjects, under the regulations of United States Food and Drug Administration (FDA) and the Department of Health and Human services, especially the Office for Human Research Protections, empower IRBs to approve and require changes in research plans prior to the initiation of research on human subjects. IRBs are regulated by Title 45 Code of Federal Regulations (CFR) Part 46 of the National Research Act of 1974. Your IRB must have at least five members. Consultants may be asked to advise IRB members.

The details and forms you must attend to will be available at your university's Office of Research Compliance or a similar body. Student complaints often center on the amount of time it takes for the IRB to respond to proposals. IRB members and the doctoral student may disagree as to what constitutes "reasonable time" for review. Questions are also sometimes raised about the issue of fit between IRB requirements and federal regulations and research differences between the humanities and the social sciences. Payments to subjects are another issue raised in some situations. Subjective judgments by the IRB as to what constitutes acceptable risks to subjects are another bone of contention at times.

We offer four things for you to consider as you move forward to get IRB approval. First, you must be able to demonstrate that there is a genuine, good faith consent process for subjects in place and subjects must be fully informed and voluntary. Second, whenever and wherever possible, put yourself in the position of a research subject and try to see through his or her eyes in order to raise questions. Third, be as patient as possible and do your best to keep minor annoyances from becoming major issues. Fourth, use your network of connections, especially your dissertation advisor and perhaps your committee members, to help you negotiate moving through this largely bureaucratic structure.

The following websites may be helpful if you seek additional information:

- Office for Human Research Protections (http://www.hhs.gov/ohrp/)
- FDA (http://www.fda.gov/)
- ICH (http://www.ich.org)
- Institutional Review Board Services (http://www.irbservices.com/)

WRITING THE FINISHED PRODUCT

Doctoral students sometimes tell us that they can't write their dissertation until they have compiled and interpreted their data. In fact, it is to your advantage to begin writing your dissertation much earlier. For example, it is wise to have potential chapter names and the kinds of information to be included in each chapter when you present your dissertation proposal.

You can also write the first chapter as well as the second chapter at the same time your data are collected. It is especially helpful if you explain the purpose and background of the research, a significant part of Chapter One, early in the game. This will alert you to the details that will need attention as your research and writing continue. As a result, drafts of chapters bearing on each phase of your research will emerge thereby rendering the final writing of your dissertation relatively simple. (See Thomas & Brubaker, 2001, p. 151.)

There are two sets of issues to be addressed in order to write the final version of your dissertation:

- Meeting the department's and university's (graduate school's) requirements as well as accommodating your dissertation committee's preferences.
- Writing a skillfully crafted, readable document.

In recent years, universities have required dissertation students to submit the final version in electronic, rather than paper, form. An example of the rationale for this requirement is in a segment from the University of North Carolina at Greensboro's website that explains the dissertation-submission process.

> An electronic dissertation is the student's original research produced, submitted, archived, and accessed in an electronic format. The components and structure

of the document are basically the same as paper dissertations. However, in the final stage, the document is converted and stored as a pdf file instead of printed and bound as a book. A pdf is a Portable Document File, created in a universal file format that allows data saved in one format to be converted into a format that can be converted into a format that can be read on any computer utilizing free Adobe Acrobat Reader.

The University of North Carolina at Greensboro, together with universities around the world, is accepting electronic dissertations (ETDs). The submission of electronic dissertations offers numerous benefits. The ETD process helps to train students in the electronic publishing and technical skills they will need as professionals. On a larger scale, the immediate and widespread availability of ETD documents provides worldwide access to scholarship. ETD's allow researchers to build on the work of those before them, even those whose work was completed in recent months, or even weeks. (Graduate School, UNCG, 2007. Further information on preparing the ETD may be found on the following website: http://www.uncg.edu/grs/cujrrent/etdabout.html).

It should be added that many professors require the submission of early drafts of dissertation chapters by e-mail for evaluation and feedback.

Advisor's Standards and Preferences

Not only must you follow departmental and university (graduate school) requirements, but you must also satisfy the standards and preferences of your major advisor and committee members. Some advisors will work with you chapter by chapter whereas others will want a completed draft of your dissertation. In any event, your advisor's support of the document is a turning point in the final stage of your dissertation research and writing. As mentioned earlier in this chapter, your advisor's credibility is also on the line when you defend your dissertation before your entire committee. There is an inherent tendency in the dissertation defense process to defer to the advisor. This tendency is only disturbed when the advisor's competence is questioned by one or more committee members.

CREATING A READABLE DOCUMENT

We define good writing as "writing that is easily and accurately understood by the audience for whom it is intended" (Thomas & Brubaker, 2008, p. 285). Your immediate audience, your dissertation committee, must judge your writing to be acceptable for you to receive the doctoral degree. However, you probably also hope that other readers—professors, graduate students, journal editors, perhaps book publishers and even informed members of the general public—will find your writing easily and accurately understandable. You are probably wise to recognize that many of the vocabulary words you use are not commonly used by many readers. You must, therefore, define them well or use more commonly understood words in their place. Both informed and uninformed audiences will appreciate precise definitions of critical words and phrases. Clarifying examples of many of your powerful ideas can be very useful.

It may be helpful to you to consider the following steps in order to "get behind the eyes" of the reader:

- Ask yourself, "If I knew nothing about this project's topic and I wanted to understand what it's all about, what questions would I want the author to answer, and how would I like to have those answers worded?"
- Ask yourself, "In my imagined role as a reader, in what sequence would I want the author to answer my questions?"
- Ask yourself, "As I consider the contents of each chapter in turn, can I identify additional, more-detailed questions for which I seek answers? If so, in what order what order can those questions profitably be addressed within the chapter?"

(For more detailed examples of answers to these questions, see Thomas & Brubaker, 2008, pp. 287–291.)

Finally, there are details about the mechanics of writing that you and your dissertation advisor must agree on before the document is sent to committee members. Given the kind of study you have done, are personal pronouns and contractions admissible? Traditionally, the answer is no, but their use is increasingly more common. Your immediate audience, your committee, must agree on such matters.

Although you may be a skilled writer, we once again wish to say that a copy editor can be useful in identifying weaknesses—"typographical errors, grammatical mistakes, the misplacement of topics, confusing explanations, undefined terms, and infelicitous phrasings" (Thomas & Brubaker, 2008, p. 296). Talk with your dissertation advisor to identify a copyeditor who has been successful in working with students who have received their doctorates. Remember that your dissertation will be a public document readily available to interested readers.

You will also want to ask your advisor to recommend one or more dissertations that have passed muster in order to see what is involved in writing an abstract for your dissertation. The abstract is a concise and precise summary of your research project—its goals and objectives, data-gathering methods, results and recommendations for further research and writing. Practical applications of the results will also frequently be identified.

Abstracts will be available in resources such as *Dissertation Abstracts International*, thus bringing attention to the importance of your research and writing. They may lead to invited presentations of your work at conferences, conventions, and other gatherings of interested parties.

ORAL DEFENSE OF THE DISSERTATION

Most doctoral students are required to defend their written document in a meeting before members of their dissertation committee. Unlike the comprehensive exams taken prior to the dissertation stage where you couldn't predict what would be asked, the oral defense of the dissertation is precisely what the phrase means—a defense of the written document that you have given to committee members. You are expected to be the expert on this topic as the research and writing you have done is uniquely your own.

Students sometimes drag their feet in scheduling their dissertation defense. This kind of procrastination can be highly detrimental to the student as it sends the message that they are not confident in the quality of their dissertation. If you have an inclination to procrastinate, share this with your advisor and ask your advisor to schedule your defense as soon as possible. Doing this may also save you an extra term or semester of tuition and fee expenses.

Difficulties that may arise during the oral defense can often be foreseen. With this in mind we turn to some difficulties and suggestions for dealing with them in a constructive way.

Presentation of Self and Setting the Stage for the Defense

It is very important that you and your advisor agree on setting the stage so that the drama that follows will lead to a successful conclusion—sign-offs by all committee members. You need to ask your advisor if non-committee members may be at the oral defense. Some departments, schools, and colleges within the university have a policy whereby faculty members have an open invitation to attend. Your advisor will also let you know if other guests may be invited by the committee to attend. It should quickly be added that non-members will not participate in the oral questioning of candidates and ensuing discussion unless they are invited to do so by the committee.

Non-members attending and you, the candidate, will also be asked to leave the room when the committee deliberates after the formal dissertation defense. When you return to the room you will be given one of the following: (1) a pass without substantive corrections after which the committee will sign formal paperwork; (2) a pass with substantive corrections to be made under the direction of your advisor with the formal paperwork signed at the defense; (3) a pass with substantive corrections to be made with committee members' signatures given after these corrections satisfy committee members, with or without a meeting of the committee; (4) a no pass, with or without the opportunity for another defense. Variations on these options may exist in your department and the university.

It is important that a meeting site be chosen that is conducive to a formal presentation and discussion of the dissertation. A seminar room with a table where materials can be spread out and easily read as well as comfortable chairs are a real plus. Appropriate electronic equipment and visual aids, such as a flip chart, should be in place. Candidates are usually asked to give a brief overview of the dissertation before questioning begins. This overview is sometimes done via power point.

Distractions, such as noise nearby, should be avoided. Some advisors will suggest that coffee and perhaps cookies can be provided. We have found, however, that more substantive food can be a real distraction that interrupts the serious nature of the defense. In one case, the candidate's family brought to the seminar room what looked like a three-course meal prior to the defense. The candidate was asked because of problems with the dissertation to consider this a planning meeting rather than a defense, the excessive amount of food was removed to the embarrassment of the candidate, and no food was served when, a few months later, the formal defense took place.

The general guideline we suggest for the candidate's presentation of self is to answer the questions briefly, to the point and stop. Natural nervousness on the part of the candidate sometimes prompts him or her to say too much, the result being that red flags are waved that don't need to be waved. As a candidate you can expect a certain amount of shuffling of papers and the like as your oral presentation begins. Simply go ahead with your presentation. One candidate, using a stern voice said that she would not begin until the committee was quiet and gave her their complete attention. The dissertation chair asked the candidate to step out of the room after telling the committee there would be a brief delay. While with the candidate in the hall, the chair told the candidate that her remarks were inappropriate, said that she should return to the room and apologize to the committee. This was done, decorum was established, and the candidate received a pass on her dissertation research and writing from committee members.

The Advisor's Role During the Dissertation Defense

Advisors are naturally somewhat nervous as their students perform at the defense. This is especially the case when the advisor isn't confident about the student's ability to handle questions. On occasion, an advisor will feel compelled to answer questions for the candidate. Committee members may openly object to such intrusions. Advisors who read this difficult situation correctly will apologize to the committee, or at least back off and not intrude again. If faced with this situation, you, the candidate, should simply be quiet as any intervention on your part will not be considered appropriate by committee members. On the few occasions when we have observed this happening, the committee and advisor have had the student's interests at heart and have worked this minor annoyance out to the satisfaction of all concerned.

Professorial Debates

Some of the best dissertation defenses we have participated in have stimulated productive debates between committee members. The best thing for you, the candidate, to do when this occurs is to listen intently in the interest of sharpening points you have made in your dissertation writing. From your viewpoint, debates can also be useful in using up 15 or 20 minutes of the two to three hour defense that would otherwise be given to grilling you. It is a rare occasion when such debates lead to ill-tempered remarks that affect the candidate. Committee members usually back off rather than create a situation that would make things difficult for the doctoral student. Once again, our advice is to answer questions precisely and concisely and then STOP. A wise advisor will also give leadership to such matters in the interest of the student.

Proper Proofreading

On rare occasions a student will submit a document that has been hastily thrown together in order to meet a university and/or department deadline. "Haste makes waste!" If the mechanics of the dissertation are not given attention, committee members may simply refuse to go forward with the defense. If the candidate conveys the feeling that mundane matters, such as spelling, grammar, and format, deserve little attention because basic ideas in the dissertation are so powerful, committee members will probably balk and be left with a very poor impression of the candidate's ability to deal with details. We experienced one defense where the candidate broke into tears and listed medical and psychological problems as a reason for a poorly constructed dissertation. The candidate said that time had run out and there would be no opportunity to clean up the dissertation given the problems experienced. The defense was in complete chaos for a half hour or so, the committee met for another hour with the student not present and the dissertation advisor said that the matter could not be resolved without extensive discussions with the candidate. The student successfully defended a few weeks later with a clean dissertation in front of each committee member.

It is obviously important, as we have pointed out throughout this book, that you have a supportive dissertation advisor and committee. With such a support system in place you will move forward and soon be addressed as Dr. _____ (fill in your last name).

Stage III

Graduation and Beyond

The Difference You Can Make Now That You Have a Doctorate

While in the doctoral program you probably looked forward at times to your career and life after having the degree in hand. The following chapter, "Reaching a Wider Audience," will serve as a kind of map or framework that will guide you so that you can consider concrete next steps after receiving the doctorate.

Maintaining and expanding your professional networks is an obvious first step. You will discover that previous contacts in your work world will view you in a somewhat different way, most graphically brought to your attention when you are introduced with a Dr. in front of your name. You will also have added many persons to your personal and professional networks during your years of doctoral study. You have, by the time you have completed your doctorate, increased your skills in relating to people and using sources of power in order to reach this important goal. (See appendix D, "The 'Table Manners' of Doctoral Student Leadership.")

As a result of these developments, you can expect opportunities to come your way. This may take place in the organization where you worked prior to beginning the doctoral program and/or a new setting. You may or may not be prepared to move to another part of the country or world to avail yourself of opportunities that interest you.

Publishing opportunities will present themselves, especially if your dissertation advisor and perhaps others see themselves as your mentors and use their networks to open doors in the publishing world. Many of these opportunities will come from your participation in professional organizations, conferences, and conventions related to your major area of doctoral study or academic discipline in general and your dissertation topic in particular. The

119

more proactive you are in pursuing these opportunities, the more publications, authored and co-authored, will follow.

Speaking opportunities will also be available in a variety of settings depending on the kinds of audiences you wish to address. Local community organizations are always on the lookout for interesting speeches, pro bono although you will often receive tokens of appreciation, such as a pen or umbrella. They provide an excellent chance to try out and hone your speaking skills.

More academic settings, such as state and national conferences and conventions, also give you the chance to share the research and writing you did on your dissertation. (See appendix I, "How Good and Comfortable Are You As a Speaker and Listener?") Reactions from the audience can be most helpful and may be included in articles and other writing you do. You may get invitations from one of more in the audience on editorial boards to submit an article to a particular journal.

Success in meeting the challenges provided by all of these situations will give you self confidence and motivation to do further research, writing, and speaking. You will also find your leadership abilities enriched by what you experienced during doctoral study thus giving you invitations and challenges to lead others in a variety of settings.

Chapter 7

Reaching a Wider Audience

On balance, will the good, the true, and the beautiful be served by what I have done? You alone must draw the final judgment of your work, no one else.

—Reid Buckley (2010, p. 67)

It is a strange feeling—having a doctorate. No one ever introduced me as Bachelor of Arts or Master of Science but now they introduce me as Doctor . . .

—A Recent Doctoral Graduate

"Write about what you know" is advice that successful writers often give to beginners. You can write best about your experiential knowledge—what you have learned from your job and your relationships.

—Allan A. Glatthorn (2002, p. 25)

The purpose of this chapter is to identify, describe, and discuss outlets you can use to reach a wider audience of persons now that you have your doctorate. Doctoral graduates sometimes share with us the exhilaration they feel in having a fresh start after years of doctoral study. They find that doors are opened that they never imagined would exist and working through the challenges these outlets offer brings new energy and discovery of talents they didn't even know they had.

PROFESSIONAL NETWORKS AS THE FOUNDATION
FOR REACHING A WIDER AUDIENCE

The professional networks you already have in place, some of which you constructed during doctoral studies, are a natural place to begin your quest for reaching a wider audience for ideas from your dissertation. In the process new career opportunities will emerge.

Networking refers to the exchange of information or services among individuals, groups or institutions in order to cultivate productive relationships. The term really came into vogue in the late 1960s. (See Brubaker, 1982, pp. 76–87.) The informal nature of networking appealed to a culture that resisted more authoritarian, bureaucratic decision-making. Today it largely focuses on the uses of computers and social relationships.

Most doctoral students acquire one or more professors who served as mentors during doctoral study and it is natural to observe how these mentors get things done in academia (see Brubaker, August, 2010, pp. 313–317). *Connections* is probably the word that describes best how your mentors achieved the success they have experienced. Your mentors would not have the senior rank and tenure they hold unless they had connections with professors and administrators who judged them to be deserving of these honors.

Your mentors would not have the research and publication records they have without connections with journal editors, professional organization editors, and book publishers. And, your mentors would not have established reputations for their writing unless readers valued their scholarship. In short, these mentors serve as models or exemplars for many of the things you wish to achieve now that you have your doctorate.

What are the qualities successful mentors have that make them successful networkers? The following attributes were cited by doctoral graduates.

- Their talents as teachers, researchers, writers, and leaders are coupled with hard work and determination to reach their goals and objectives.
- They are highly accomplished as individuals and also know how to work with others as co-workers and members of groups and teams.
- They honor the civilities of relationships and leadership.
- They know how to take care of themselves and others in difficult situations.
- They care about and help others whom they respect as evidenced by what they have done with and for you. They have the air of authority and use this to nurture and guide you (Levinson, 1978, p. 123).
- Their values and commitments are clearly observable in their behaviors and yet they know when to compromise in order to get "a piece of the pie."

- They love their work and clearly want to do what they are doing in the world of work. They recognize the distinction between a vocation, sense of calling, and a job.
- They prize learning and share this love for learning with others, including you.
- They not only take but seize opportunities to make things happen for themselves and others.
- They recognize the need for space for those being mentored so that they can become their own persons, even to the extent that the mentoring relationship may no longer be needed by the person being mentored (Levinson, 1978, pp. 147, 251–256; Nouwen, 1986, p. 71).
- They understand the systems in which they operate, knowing how people are invested and how they can benefit from it.
- They are hungry for new ideas and are quick to recognize the talents of others.

Each of your mentors has a combination of some of these qualities and draws on them to different degrees of intensity in different contexts. It is the way in which they do this that makes their mentoring styles unique. It is the uniqueness of their mentoring that makes each one stand out in your mind as you reflect on how they influenced you. When you describe this influence to others you probably tell one or more stories, for it is narratives that capture best how mentors make a difference in our lives.

We should quickly add that many of you also acquired mentors outside of the university during doctoral study and at other times during your career. Many of these people are probably more involved in leadership activities and less involved in academic research and writing. Most of the qualities assigned to professors as mentors also hold for these mentors. Given the important role of mentors and what they taught you about professional networking, what guidelines for building and maintaining professional networks will be useful in furthering your career and making your life more productive and enjoyable?

Answers to this question will depend on where you are at this time in your career and where you want to be in the immediate and more distant future. Some of you have gone straight through higher education programs, including the doctorate, and are at the beginning stage of your career. Others have had one or more careers before receiving your doctorate. Within this group some of you will want to stay on the same career path, whereas others will want to start a new career. Some of our doctoral graduates describe themselves as "place-bound" whereas others are more mobile. We begin our discussion with a look at higher education opportunities.

The World of Higher Education

Our doctoral students often refer to the doctoral diploma as the "union card" that will give them access to the professoriate. They frequently say they would like to return to the university where they earned their doctorate as a full-time faculty member, an unlikely event given universities reluctance to hire their own graduates, especially in tenure-track positions.

Pressure on colleges and universities to hire professors who have an earned doctorate has come from many quarters: accrediting agencies; magazines, such as *U.S. News and World Report*, and organizations that rank institutions, as well as their major study areas; and parents and alumni who associate having a doctorate with increasing the prestige of the institution.

The various kinds of doctorates held by faculty members, such as Ph.D., Ed.D. and others with their professional affiliations attached to them, may or may not be advertised by institutions of higher education, but the few extremely prestigious universities that award doctorates are often named when a faculty member's doctorate is cited, particularly at the hiring stage. This is especially the case in alumni magazines and other popular forms of communication that advertise the college or university.

It is to your advantage as a doctoral graduate who is considering entering the professoriate to know what faculty and administrative positions are available and what is expected of you in order to successfully advance your career. The first thing to note is that positions may be divided into two general areas: tenure track and non-tenure track. Non-tenure track appointments are for a fixed period of time, often from a semester to a few years, with no guarantee for employment beyond this contractual agreement. Examples are titles such as instructor, lecturer, visiting professor, clinical professor, adjunct professor, and the like. Research and writing are not required in such roles and released time for research and writing is not provided.

Tenure-track positions put you in line for a lifetime appointment, subject to dismissal only on grounds of moral turpitude or elimination of an area of study within the institution once tenure is granted. Tenure is usually linked to the associate professorship and full professorship, although new hires at the associate professor level are increasingly not given tenure.

Research and writing are considerations in the granting of tenure, promotion to a higher rank, and the awarding of merit money. This is especially the case in doctorate-granting universities. A major reason given for this is that professors who do research and writing serve as a model for dissertation students and are in a better position to help these students at the dissertation research and writing stage as it is assumed they are up on the most recent research and their writing skills are sharp.

This brings us to a description of a current trend some disciplines employ in the evaluation of tenure-track professors' writing (Cohen, August 24, 2010, pp. 1 and 3). This trend relies on peer review. A review committee, often called the Tenure and Promotion Committee, whose members have tenure and a rank higher than the candidate, sends the professor's writing to a limited number of professors outside the institution, professors considered experts in the field of study in which the article, monograph or book is written.

Reviewers are usually anonymous. This can take a few months or more, thus slowing down the tenure and/or promotion committees' deliberations. Assistant professors, new to these matters of delay on the part of editors and publishers in bringing publications to print and tenure and promotion committees' slowness in getting experts' reactions to publications when they are in print, must be aware of these realities in the tenure and promotion process.

The new method, often referred to as open review, invites online readers to comment on journal articles, monographs, and books in progress, thus giving the review committee responses from a broader community in a more timely manner. Journal editorial boards would use the same open review process to decide what should and should not be published in journals. If this process is familiar to you, you may recognize it as one used by *Wikipedia*. As one might assume, the process is as controversial in academia as *Wikipedia* itself.

A combination of these two methods may well be used by review committees in the future, thus bringing to this process an inclusiveness and transparency not found in the traditional way of doing business.

Doctoral graduates will note that there are several trends in higher education during difficult economic times that affect employment opportunities and the nature of your work environment. First, many colleges and universities are now hiring more professors in non-tenure track positions. This gives these institutions the opportunity to pay less for faculty members' salaries and not make long-range commitments to areas of study that may have decreased enrollments in the future.

If you are hired for such positions, the effect is for you to be in a holding position, much as an airplane waiting to land. This works in your favor only if you don't wish to make a commitment to an institution, or your choice is between this job and no job.

Second, with fewer tenure-track or line positions available and many more applicants than in the past, those tenure-track positions that are available will often entail your being appointed as an administrator of a program or a unit of the college or university along with your other professorial activities, such as teaching, advising, research, and service in the department, school, college, and university. The effect of this is that you will have less time to do research and writing, activities that are major keys to promotion and tenure.

While serving as an administrator of a program, you may well be expected to write successful proposals for funding. (See Achilles & Brewer, 2008; and Glatthorn, 2002, pp. 212–222.) There are limited occasions when professors involved in writing grant proposals and administering large programs where grant money is in place have received tenure for such efforts. Universities are afraid that the grants are so linked to the professor that the grant may leave with the professor as he or she joins another institution of higher education.

Furthermore, it is not guaranteed that you will be promoted and tenured for securing even a major grant. For this reason, it is recommended that those in tenure-track positions consult with their tenure and promotion policies, administrators, and colleagues. In many cases, grants provide opportunities for research and writing that would not be available otherwise. Just as you sought multiple payoffs for activities in your doctoral program, you will likely benefit in similar ways while a new faculty member.

Third, any teaching may well require computer skills that will allow you to teach online courses. Such courses save the university a considerable amount of money as there is no need for classroom space, heating and cooling of such space, and travel expenses for professors if courses were to have been held off-campus. Alternatively, online courses can be costly for universities that have little expertise in this area as training and technical support requires additional financial resources. For all of these reasons, your sophisticated technology skills may be a very positive factor in the hiring process.

REACHING A WIDER AUDIENCE THROUGH SPEAKING AND WRITING

Wherever you are on your career path after earning and receiving your doctorate, whether in higher education or elsewhere, you will be encouraged by your dissertation advisor, committee members and others to build on your dissertation research and writing to reach a wider audience. You will use your professional networks already in place and also add to them in order to reach this wider audience. You will use your speaking and writing skills, often in tandem, to share and extend ideas from your dissertation. There are several publishing outlets that will help you reach this goal. (See Thomas & Brubaker, 2008, pp. 309–322; and Brubaker, 2006, pp. 17–28.)

Presentations at Conferences

Many doctoral programs encourage and provide support for doctoral students to attend seminars and colloquia with peers and faculty members. These experiences introduce students to the culture of conferences. We encourage you to give special attention at conferences, such as those sponsored by the American Educational Research Association (AERA), the American Psychological Association (APA), and the like, to presentations by recent doctoral graduates.

Formats at conferences may include lectures, panels, discussion groups, question and answer sessions, debates and poster presentations. The latter is the more recent innovation of these formats, with researchers displaying key elements of their work that invite generally informal discussion with their creators. The size of the audience varies according to the popularity of the topic, the reputation of the presenter(s), the time of day and competing sessions. (See appendix I, "How Good and Comfortable Are You As a Speaker and Listener?")

You may find it disturbing but inevitable that some people will walk in and out during your presentation. A colleague turned to us during such a time and said, "It looks like they are voting with their feet!" Free materials are often distributed so that you can pick them up even though you stay for a brief period of time.

Sometimes papers are placed on tables in hallways thus giving easy access to such papers for those not attending sessions. Some participants, who don't go through normal review channels and aren't listed in program brochures, leave papers they've written on tables and make the following entry on their resumes: _____ (paper title) *delivered* at the Conference on _____, on such and such a date. This is one of those secrets that is rarely discussed.

The opportunity to have your research paper accepted for delivery at a conference is much greater than having it accepted for publication in a journal or as a book chapter. Papers are frequently co-authored by a number of persons, the result being that one co-author may be at one session as a presenter while others are speaking in another part of the conference building(s) at the same time. Frequently the opportunity to be a presenter is limited to members of the professional organization that sponsors the conference.

A few words about public speaking may be helpful to you as you consider conferences and the like. There is no one right speaking style. It therefore makes sense that the starting place is to know what kind of person you basically are. Are you more comfortable and proficient in speaking to small groups or large gatherings of people?

Some speakers favor an informal presentation style in small group settings whereas others prefer a more formal speaking style, such as reading a paper, behind a lectern in front of large groups of people. We should add that simply reading a paper can put the audience to sleep and yet this method of delivery persists.

Knowing your preferred speaking style and settings makes it more likely that you will give an authentic or genuine presentation. The audience will perceive you as sincere, a "person who believes in the impression fostered by your own performance" (Goffman, 1959, p. 18).

Regardless of your style, the secret is to focus on the audience, rather than yourself, and share your warmth with them. One good way to focus on the audience is to think about how curious you are to learn more about them and their reactions to your ideas. You will discover that "it's this desire for contact, to make something happen, that gives a speaker energy" (Linver, 1978, p. 41). One way to share your warmth is to share your sense of humor. This has the effect of relaxing the audience, whether it is one person or 100. Stories or narratives are also excellent ways to get and keep the audience's attention.

The physical setting in which you speak sets the stage for your speaking. In both formal and informal settings, it can be useful to have a mental checklist. For example, remove distractions, such as a gurgling coffeepot; have chairs and/or tables arranged the way you want them; assess acoustics and check equipment; and have a resume for the person who is introducing you. Your preparation sends the message that you care enough about the audience to have done your homework. All of these things affect the dynamics of the setting and also give you, the speaker, a sense of security.

You will naturally be nervous to some extent before speaking in many situations. Treat this nervousness as a good thing, for it means that you care enough about the audience and yourself to get psyched up for the occasion. Self-talk can be helpful as you prepare: "Good going. I have an edge on and I know that this is necessary in order to do a good job." It is especially helpful to realize that the audience wants you to succeed and is therefore with you from the start.

Success breeds success and gives your presentation an optimistic tone, something the audience will appreciate. The challenge is to be interesting to your audience *and* yourself. When you meet this challenge you will experience one of the feelings associated with success: You and the audience will have an interest connection, a sense of oneness. When you reach this place you will be in the zone, a place we call *comfortable competence*.

All of these suggestions are examples of what Erving Goffman calls *impression management* (Goffman, 1959). How do you get better in speaking situations? Practice . . . practice . . . practice. "Winston Churchill was asked what he did in his spare time. He responded, 'I rehearse my extemporaneous speeches" (Adams, 1983, p. 229).

Academic Journals

There are thousands of academic journals, most of which are quarterly. Subject-matter focus may be on an academic journal (*American Anthropologist*), a region (*Georgia Historical Society*), a sociogeographic entity (*Education and*

Urban Society), a professional specialization (*The American Music Teacher*), an ethnic group (*Journal of Black Studies*), a gender category (*Women's Studies Quarterly*), and a religious affiliation or denomination (*Christian Century*).

Rather obviously, the larger the membership in the society, the larger the guaranteed readership. Cost is a key issue in order to keep a journal alive, particularly in recent years where library funds have been diminished.

The most prestigious and popular journals may accept as few as 5 percent or 10 percent of papers submitted. Lower status journals may accept as many as 70 percent or more. Journals are also measured by the average number of times their articles are cited by other journals, often called the *impact factor*. The higher impact journals are frequently the more prestigious in which to publish. Time lag and efficiency in dealing with authors' submissions vary a good deal from journal to journal.

Acceptable lengths of articles are described in journals' guidelines for submission of papers. These guidelines may be found online after searching for the name of the journal. They are sometimes described in the front of journals. Increasingly, many journals provide a service for online submission and for letting authors track their article, once accepted, through the production process.

Once a paper is accepted, the editor will inform you what revisions need to be made by such and such a date. It is wise to get right on with such revisions as it indicates your positive view of the journal and its editor(s).

Some journals are referred to as refereed, this meaning that the paper is sent to a few persons considered experts who evaluate the paper for its contribution to knowledge and quality of its research and writing. Reviews of papers are often called blind reviews as names of authors are removed from the manuscripts. In case of mixed reviews the paper may be sent out for further reviews. Several months are usually involved in this whole process of getting a paper published in an academic journal. Patience is the order of the day, although difficult at times to maintain.

Some journals only accept invited papers. Although most journals do not charge authors for publication of papers, some may require that authors contribute to the expense of the publication, usually a given amount per printed page. Two or three courtesy copies are given to authors.

Journal editors naturally want authors and their readers to perceive the review process as objective. However, editors have a good deal of discretionary power and it is hard to believe, for example, that a respected scholar who has published with prestigious journals previously will not be given special consideration.

And, it is simply a fact that writers use people in their networks to give them special advantages. It is also true that authors who are easy to get along with and engage in the civilities of getting along with others will be given

certain advantages. Notes of appreciation to editors can make a real difference as they are rarely received. In short, the review process is a human
endeavor. Every established author has interesting stories to tell that make
this point.

Popular and Trade Periodicals

When the term *popular periodicals* is used, it refers to magazines, newsletters
and newspapers read by the general public. *Trade periodicals* are similar in
the production process as popular periodicals; however, their audience is the
set of professionals within that trade. For instance, the *Monitor on Psychology* would be considered a trade periodical, a magazine format that is delivered to all with an APA membership.

Neither popular nor trade periodicals are considered peer reviewed journals
and often have less prestige, especially in the tenure and promotion process.
Both types of publications can be valuable nonetheless, especially when considering various audiences you wish to reach. Additionally, you often have
greater flexibility in formatting and writing style for these publications, as
they are generally less technical in nature.

You will sometimes be asked by the editor to write an article whereas on
other occasions you will initiate contact with the editor. Articles are usually
briefer than those in academic journals, and language is adjusted to speak to
the general public. Editors frequently simplify sentences to use limited space.
Sometimes an author is paid, but usually the publication believes that your
wide distribution of the article is reward enough in itself. An airline's inflight
magazine editor, for example, paid one of the present book's co-authors
fifty dollars for each article co-authored. When asked about this, the editor
responded, "You should have paid us for the exposure. We reach thousands
of people each day!"

A major advantage of writing in popular periodicals is the wide readership.
For example, a Sunday edition of a major newspaper reaches thousands of
homes. Some articles written for popular periodicals can be expanded into chapters for books and the like. This is also true for articles written for newspapers.

Books

Books are usually described as one of two types—trade and academic.
Trade books are written for the general public and will be found in regular
bookstores and public libraries. Academic books are written for specialized
audiences like students and faculty members in higher education institutions,
teachers and administrators in schools, attorneys, doctors, and the like.

They are advertised increasingly online and are found in libraries of higher education institutions, college and university bookstores, and academic publishers' catalogs. If successful they may reach bestseller lists in publications like the *New York Times.*

Popular trade books are frequently not accepted by publishers. Authors therefore hire agents to deal with publishers. Several friends who have hired agents say that it is simply a waste of money as their agents did a lot for themselves and little, if anything, for their authors.

Scholarly manuscripts are usually accepted by book publishers, but chances of acceptance are enhanced if recommended by an established author who knows the publisher. This person may write a foreword for your book thus bringing attention to its value. If you have not published a book before, you would be wise to seek the counsel of an established academic author who will fill you in on what needs to be done to have your manuscript or book outline seriously considered by a publisher.

You will discover that each book publisher will have its own list of guidelines you will be required to follow in order to get your manuscript accepted for publication. These guidelines are frequently listed online.

It is simply a fact that this manuscript that you want turned into a book is "your baby," and you believe it to be priceless and beautiful. Given the large number of manuscripts received by acquisitions editors, they often view your work as another item in a pile on their desk or the floor.

A friend, who was a newly hired professor in a northern university, had lunch with an acquisitions editor in the middle of winter. On their way back to the university after lunch the editor's car got stuck in the snow. The editor, to the great surprise and angst of our friend, opened his trunk, took out book manuscripts to be reviewed, put them under the tires of his rental car for traction out of the snow and drove off.

In most cases academic book production costs are paid by the publisher. A typical author royalty is 10 percent of actual cash received by the publisher. Only when a book becomes a widely purchased textbook does the author receive a significant amount of money. However, an author can indirectly receive payoff in higher education positions if the publication of a book is factored into promotions, tenure and merit increases.

The time lag between initial submission of manuscript to publication of the book can vary from almost a year to several years depending on the efficiency of the editorial staff and your response as an author to necessary revisions. Some delays, such as receiving permission to quote from copyrighted passages from other books and the backlog of manuscripts waiting to be printed, will factor into time lag. Forms for such permissions are usually online under the publisher's name. (See Glatthorn, 2002, pp. 142–157.)

Chapters in Books

Shorter versions of your dissertation or newly written material may be used as a chapter in a book. This can give your ideas exposure that would not otherwise take place. Promising responses to your chapter may result in a longer term writing project, such as a monograph or book. There are three means by which your chapter will be published.

First, a person in your network of contacts invites authors to write chapters for a book on a subject of his or her choosing. The person who initiates contact with you will write introductory material and probably also include one or more chapters in this volume. The book may or may not have an index. An index can, however, be helpful to readers.

Second, an editor selects already published journal articles or excerpts from books already published. If you have published an article, it may be a candidate for this kind of book. This if often referred to in the title or subtitle as a book of readings.

Third, papers presented at one or more conferences are compiled in a book. As with other edited books, publishers and the editor of the book often consider authors to be in a position to increase sales of the book.

Editors of books like those just described are challenged to get invited chapters in on time, edit material so that it becomes clean copy, and negotiate with publishers for a contract. In short, there is a good deal of challenging detail work to be done, something that you should consider if you are interested in editing a volume.

Chapter writers who are procrastinators are a special problem, and you may well invest a good deal of time and energy getting them to do their work. It can be very helpful to you to know the writer's track record with regard to promptness before inviting him or her to be a contributor in the book.

Authors of chapters receive a free copy of the book when it is published and occasionally get a minimal one-time flat fee or low percentage of the editor's royalty money. Most of the time the chapter author's payoff is exposure and perhaps positive consideration for promotions, tenure, and salary increases. There is, however, considerable satisfaction in seeing something of your own in print. As one author said, "We all leave footprints in life and publishing is one of the most visible of such footprints." You can return to the printed page in the future and be proud of your contribution.

Electronic and Live Presentations

Recorded reports of research projects, including dissertations, are sometimes broadcast on radio and television or presented directly to audiences of students and others in classrooms and at conferences. Exciting ways of using the

Internet and World Wide Web are also being used to disseminate research results.

The role of researchers, if any, in producing and distributing electronic presentations varies. Research grants and institutional support sometimes exists for the support of such presentations but in many cases the costs of the work must be borne by researchers themselves.

Recorded and live radio and television presentations may take the form of news spots, talk-show appearances and special programs. The following guidelines for going on television are in checklist format and may be useful to you given today's 24/7 news coverage (Brubaker, 2006, pp. 26–27).

1. Talk to the reporter, not the camera or microphone. (Look the reporter straight in the eye.)
2. Stand or sit erectly. Don't stoop or bend over.
3. If you say, "No comment," add that you will get back to the reporter in such and such a time.
4. Know who you're dealing with and develop rapport with the reporter when possible.
5. Remember the photographer (cameraperson) doesn't have the camera to his or her eye. The camera can be rolling from any position, even if it is under his or her arm.
6. Be politely on guard all of the time.
7. Take advantage of the nonconfrontational good news programs.
8. The bottom line is to meet reporters head-on and be honest. The camera doesn't lie. It will see the eyes.
9. Be cool and confident. It disarms reporters.
10. Remember that there is a high degree of sensitivity about minorities and women at this time in the history of our nation.
11. A smile is the most disarming thing in the world. Bring to the camera the real person inside you.
12. Be prepared. If you don't know, say, "I don't know."
13. There is no such thing as "off the record." Beware of the reporter who says, "This is off the record."
14. You can ask to talk to the reporter about something before you go on camera. If the reporter won't allow you to do this, don't talk.
15. It is a good idea to suggest a place for the interview. Get an appropriate visual backdrop.
16. Watch hazards around you. Don't swivel in a chair. Don't fidget. Calm down, even if it means you grab a desk in front of you or behind you.
17. Take your time.
18. Ask to reshoot if you are extremely dissatisfied with the interview.

19. Limit the number of remarks and focus on two or three major points.
20. Ask the reporter both whom he or she has talked to and whom he or she will talk to before the story is out.
21. You can occasionally stop a reporter dead in his or her tracks by saying, "I have no earthly idea what you're talking about."
22. The place where you are being interviewed may be private property. Be aware, however, that television cameras can shoot onto your property from a nearby site without your permission.

It is obvious that there are a number of opportunities for you to get reactions to your research and writing in general and your dissertation in particular by using electronic and in-person presentations. You will sharpen your ideas and presentation-of-self skills and in the process discover new ideas for writing.

Internet Publishing

The fast growth of the Internet and World Wide Web has created a new outlet for research reports, including your dissertation. The increasingly expensive cost of getting work in print and widely disseminated has turned people to new electronic outlets.

If you are new to internet publishing, one of the best places to start is a website called *Learn the Net: Web Publishing* at the following World Wide Web address: www.learnthenet.com/english/section/webpubl.html. Services like USENET (users' network) accept your dissertation abstract and place it on the bulletin board that could reach millions of people.

A second option is to transmit your manuscript via the internet to one of the electronic journals and magazines, such as *Current Research in Social Psychology*. University libraries can furnish you with the names of electronic periodicals for publishing your dissertation or an abbreviated version of it.

A third outlet is to create your own web page where you can post your dissertation, research reports and the like. Software packages like Dream Weaver, NetObjects Fusion and Netscape Composer can help you create a website.

A fourth option is to have your dissertation published as an *e-book* (electronic book) posted on the Internet. Publishing services will issue your book to people who buy it in electronic form to be read on a computer screen.

Turn-around time is quick with electronic publishing and your work can be revised easily and efficiently. You can also receive quick feedback from readers via e-mail. And, you have complete control over the form of the report. The disadvantage, in contrast to working with a publisher, is that you will not get the help of a copyeditor and proofreader. It is worth the investment to talk to established authors about who they used as copyeditors and pay an excellent copyeditor to work on your manuscript.

Researcher-Created Print Publications

Desktop publishing, with an up-to-date word-processing program, allows a researcher to create book or journal pages that appear to be professionally typeset. A good photocopy machine can be used to print copies for dissemination to persons in the author's network. The disadvantages of this are that the author has to find a competent copyeditor and proofreader, and your network for disseminating the work is probably quite limited.

All of the detail work done by publishing companies is probably not at your disposal. Finally, this way of publishing may well be viewed as vanity publishing for the checks and controls established by publishers are probably not in place. Resources for advertising your work are unlikely to exist in contrast to established resources available to publishing companies.

Finally, we have examined many publishing outlets for your research and writing and are left with the question, "Why should I write?" As you know from doing your dissertation, there are times when you feel like you are on the wings of angels while writing and there are other times when you experience bumps in a long and difficult road. As with any creative endeavor, hard work and self-discipline are an essential part of the process. The better you write the more the reader will view your writing as easy for you to do.

We highly recommend that you read Reid Buckley's *This Business of Writing: What to Avoid, What to Do, How to Get It Down.* He has been teaching good prose through his School of Thought, Reflection and Communications in South Carolina for twenty-five years. Among his students were Philip Roth. J. D. Salinger, Norman Mailer, William Manchester, Toni Morrison, Stephen King and Danielle Steele, all of whom used pseudonyms when they came to him for instruction. As you read his book you will begin to answer the question raised in the first line of this paragraph. You will find his book and any contact you have with him inspirational, as it has been for us. His sense of humor and competence are a gift to all of us.

Appendixes

We have developed a number of appendixes that may be read and reacted to privately or in a group setting. We encourage you to discuss your reactions to these appendixes with members of your support network, including fellow doctoral students. They can provide honest feedback and serve as a sounding board for your ideas. Dissertation seminar professors and those who teach introductory doctoral level courses can use the appendixes as instructional tools. These courses are often designed to help orient students to doctoral programs.

We invite you to e-mail us so that we can converse with each other as you use these appendixes: michael.brubaker@uc.edu and dlbrubak@uncg.edu. We promise a response.

Appendix A

Bringing Coherence to the Body of Work You've Done in Preparation for Doctoral Study

Work, the exertion of effort to accomplish something you think is important, is an essential part of life. In considering going for a doctorate, it can be useful to look back at the body of work you have done in order to assess lessons learned and identify the talents or abilities you have drawn upon in order to capitalize on opportunities that have come your way. By doing so you will be better able to find a doctoral program that will meet your needs and desires to experience what Malcolm Gladwell (2008), author of *Outliers: The Story of Success,* calls "the miracle of meaningful work" (p. 269).

The point is that you can help write your own script for success, in this case earning a doctorate, by choosing a doctoral program that will afford you opportunities to use your analytical and practical intelligence. Preparation and hard work will give you what sociologists call "accumulative advantage" (Gladwell, 2008, p. 30).

The lessons you have learned, the body of work you have experienced, come from formal and informal settings. Seymour B. Sarason (1972) defines a setting as "*any* instance when two or more people come together in new and sustained relationships to achieve certain goals" (p. ix). We ask you to keep in mind the distinction between formal and informal settings as you begin to identify lessons you have learned and talents you have used. Lessons learned and talents used always take place within a context or setting.

Please imagine a situation in which you are attending a day-long seminar sponsored by a doctoral program in a nearby university. The seminar is designed to introduce you to the program. The director of the program briefly describes the program and then surprises the small group by saying that you don't enter a program as a blank slate but rather have a wealth of experiences that have helped prepare you for doctoral study. You are asked to pair off with a partner in order to answer two questions: "What are three things you have learned that you believe you can build on to successfully complete a doctoral program? And, where did you learn each of these things?" You have forty-five minutes for this discussion.

What will you say to your partner, knowing full well that you will probably be asked to share your own or your partner's answers with the small group when it convenes?

Lesson Learned	Context
1.	
2.	
3.	

An example of a student's response follows:

Lesson Learned	Context
1. Intelligence will only take me so far. At this point other things, like hard work, focus and a sense of purpose, are primary.	I was less than satisfied with some of the papers I wrote and I sometimes received a B on papers that could have been an A.
2. Writing is the most nearly perfect academic thing I can do.	When I took the time to copy edit and proofread papers, I had a sense of accomplishment and received more favorable comments from professors and better grades.
3. Not even the best of students makes it alone.	Fierce independence left me with a sense of loneliness and few real friends—too high a price to pay.

What *coherence*, sense of connectedness or pattern of thinking and behaving, is there in the prospective doctoral student's response? In order to move forward and successfully complete the doctoral program, the doctoral student needs to focus on applied intelligence, not simply analytical intelligence. The student also needs to continue to value writing excellence by writing several drafts after copyediting and proofreading. And, the student needs to privately and publicly recognize and act upon the role others play in his work and life.

Appendix B

Selecting a Doctoral Program

Please write a number from 1 (low) to 5 (high) on the following items that influence/influenced your decision in selecting a doctoral program. You are encouraged after each item to add further comments that will be useful to you and others in discussion sessions.

_____1. Tuition cost. Elaborate:

_____2. Other expenses: e.g., housing, food, travel. Elaborate:

_____3. Geographical location and/or proximity. Elaborate:

_____4. Prestige of university. Elaborate:

_____5. Prestige of doctoral program. Elaborate:

_____6. Full-time option. Elaborate:

_____7. Part-time option. Elaborate:

_____8. Availability of online courses. Elaborate:

_____9. Entrance consideration given to previous work experience. Elaborate:

_____10. Entrance consideration given to previous grade point average. Elaborate:

_____11. Entrance consideration given to standardized test scores. Elaborate:

_____12. Opportunity to make the case for your being admitted to program. Elaborate:

_____13. Quality of faculty. Elaborate:

_____14. Availability of personal attention to students. Elaborate:

_____15. Availability of mentors in your area of interest. Elaborate:

_____16. Opportunities for scholarships, fellowships, assistantships. Elaborate:

_____17. Helpfulness of program's clerical staff in handling your inquiries. Elaborate:

_____17. Doctoral program's emphasis on new technologies. Elaborate:

_____18. Physical facilities in which program is housed. Elaborate:

_____19. Way in which you were treated in visiting university and department. Elaborate:

_____20. Program's reputation for placing students after graduation. Elaborate:

Appendix C

The Power of Critique

Your ability to critique is an essential part of scholarship in doctoral study. It is sometimes defined as the art or practice of criticism but it can be much more than this deficit definition that focuses on what is wrong or missing. Critique occurs when you (a) review what has taken place, (b) adopt a point of view (thesis) as to what took place, and (c) support this point of view or thesis. It is important that we find the goodness, what goes right, as we are involved in critique while at the same time addressing problems to be solved and dilemmas to be reconciled. You will see the importance of this balance in the examples that follow.

You participated in the art of critique in Appendix A, Bringing Coherence to the Body of Work You've Done in Preparation for Doctoral Study. You reviewed the work you've done in your life. This review included *discernment*, separating the less important from the more important, in order to identify lessons learned. These lessons reflected one or more points of view (theses) that you then supported. Making such a judgment or judgments always depended on the particular *context* in which significant events took place. For example, you learned from comments and less than excellent grades by some teachers and professors that copy editing and proofreading were necessary steps in writing better papers. We have discovered as professors who expect and in fact demand copy editing and proofreading that students are surprised and sometimes angry with us for enforcing these scholarly norms whereas some previous teachers and professors didn't have these expectations while at the same time giving students only positive comments and grades on their writings. Once students accept the reality of the new context they are usually disappointed and angry with previous teachers and professors.

In doctoral study you will see that critique is a central process in writing papers and doing dissertation research and writing. For example, reviewing literature, when done well, depends on a discerning eye and adopting a point of view with regard to its value, supported by evidence. It is much more than a list of sources that serves as filler. Critique will also play a key role in your verbal exchanges in class, your oral defense of your written comprehensive examination and your dissertation defense.

We have discovered that once doctoral students become familiar with critique they find it one of the most enjoyable scholarly tools in the doctoral experience. It can be a playful as well as a serious part of the communication process.

Appendix D

The "Table Manners" of Doctoral Student Leadership

When you enter the culture of doctoral studies, you become party to a kind of covenant with your professors. There are norms that serve as civilities in this culture. The variety of backgrounds, talents, interests and aspirations provides a richness important to your personal growth. Professors, university administrators, and others are a vehicle to assist you with your learning. The following guidelines are designed to facilitate clear doctoral student—professor communication and enhance leadership skills and attitudes. Please use a magic marker to highlight the guidelines and ideas that speak to you. Then, if possible, please use these guidelines to stimulate discussion.

Basic assumptions faculty often bring to this process:

- Doctoral students should play a proactive role, not simply a reactive one.
- As part of doctoral program planning, students should be familiar with the program's guidelines, rules, and regulations.
- If a substantive reaction to student writing is called for on the part of a professor, doctoral students should negotiate this well in advance.
- When a student submits a written document, electronic or hard copy, clean copy is required. Use a good copy editor or proofreader to ensure this.
- Open communication, rather than "hidden agendas," is the key to mutual respect and consideration.
- The scholarly responsibility a student assumes in preparation for and in reacting in class is an important responsibility assumed in class.
- Effective oral and written communication is a key to successful doctoral student leadership in the doctoral program and beyond.
- Removing and minimizing "irritants" lead to a better relationship with professors.

- As part of the negotiation process, doctoral students and professors should clearly state their expectations. You will soon learn that patience and the art of negotiation are essential to good relationships with your advisor and committee members.

If you want satisfaction as a doctoral student:

- Be sure to ask for the professor's e-mail address if this is not in the course syllabus.
- With regard to telephone calls to the instructor, if the professor isn't in, leave your name, telephone number, the nature of your business, and the best time to return your call.
- For efficient and effective use of your time, prepare for the content of the telephone conversation.
- Identify yourself at the onset of the conversation on the phone.
- When substantive agreements are arrived at over the telephone, the doctoral student should follow up with an e-mail or memorandum of understanding concluding with "Unless I hear from you otherwise, I'll assume this is correct."
- Don't have secretaries, in the event that you have one, place calls to professors that put faculty members on hold until the caller is available to talk.
- Remember to save appropriate parties' e-mails or memoranda.
- In some cases, give a self-addressed, stamped envelope to the professor for a sure response. Log important contacts, electronically or with hard copy, with date, time, and outline of content in your log.
- Clearly state what you expect of the professor when communicating with him or her.
- It is probably wise to use a fairly formal style when e-mailing an instructor.
- Don't assume e-mail communication is private.
- Since there are a number of ways to communicate with your advisor, ask which communication method is preferred. You will soon learn from direct experiences with your advisor and others and/or advice from "the grapevine" if professors are comfortable with and approve of abbreviated forms of communication, such as texting.
- When there is agreement on a due date, be sure to meet this date unless extenuating circumstances arrive. If this happens, let your advisor know as soon as possible and set another due date. Be sure this doesn't happen repeatedly.
- When a book, article, speech or the like really speaks to you and your interests, contact the author or speaker to express your appreciation and explain why the author or speaker made a difference in your life. This is seldom done and highly appreciated. The author or speaker will frequently

provide other sources important to your scholarship. If you cite the author or speaker in your research and writing, you may wish to ask the author or speaker if he or she would like a copy of your work. This often leads to meaningful communication.

- Some students find it helpful to keep a running record or journal of thoughts and feelings during the doctoral program and/or dissertation process. This may be done electronically or with hard copy. You can return to these entries from time to time and highlight ideas that may be useful to present-day needs and desires.
- Some students have had considerable success in selecting small seminars and independent studies to get better acquainted with professors' professional interests and expertise hone their own research and writing skills. Use your doctoral student network to investigate this matter.

Appendix E

Dealing with Contradictions
in a Doctoral Program

Arthur M. Schlesinger, Jr. (2000) notes that conflict, freedom, change, and discovery are essential ingredients in a democracy:

> So long as society stays free, so long will it continue in a state of tension, breeding *contradiction*, breeding strife. But, conflict is also the guarantee of freedom; it is the instrument of change; it is above all, the source of discovery, the source of art, the source of love (pp. 521–522; italics ours).

Contradiction comes from the Latin *contra* (against) + *dicere* or *dictus* (to say). For our purposes, contradiction is the act of saying or doing the opposite of something already said or done.

Two kinds of contradictions facing the doctoral student are the basis for the following exercise. These contradictions are (1) those one chooses to celebrate and (2) those one chooses to try to reconcile. (We talk about problem *solving* and dilemma *reconciling*. With the latter, you simply live with the issue as best you can.)

Please identify those contradictions that you face or might face as a doctoral student to be celebrate and those you choose to try to reconcile in a doctoral program.

Column 1 (celebrate)	Column 2 (reconcile)
One of my professors is younger than I am but the professor's rich experiences and excellent teaching, research and writing are admirable and helpful.	I feel, as a part-time student that I have one foot in my job during the day, the other in night classes.
I celebrate my abilities as a doctoral student but have learned not to say much about them.	My professors respect my confidence as a scholar. Students don't.

149

Appendix F

Working Alone and Working
As a Team Member

As you make your way through the doctoral program, you will experience the democratic tenets of valuing autonomy (working alone) and working as a part of a team. It is a challenge in both of these situations to find the most satisfying balance between these two ways of operating. Please complete the following sentences:

There are times when I enjoy working alone. Some of these times are . . .

Some of the reasons why I enjoy working alone are . . .

There are times when I prefer working with others as a member of a team. Some of these times are . . .

Some of the reasons why I enjoy working as a team member are . . .

How do you know when you are an effective team member? Please highlight the items that speak to this question.

- I recognize that what I do affects others on the team as well as those the team influences.
- No one on the team projects the feeling that he or she is better than others.
- I am privately and publicly willing to acknowledge other team members' talents and contributions.
- I rarely feel lonely.
- I rarely feel down but instead feel lifted up by team members.
- I feel energized.
- I discover resources that I didn't know I had.
- I have the courage to do what I think is right.
- My vision for the future is sharpened, thus motivating myself and others.
- I can agree and disagree with fellow team members without taking this personally.
- I feel free to try out or practice ideas and skills while having a safety net of support.
- I am encouraged to take risks that I otherwise would be reluctant to take.
- People with more status than I have encourage and reward me for being a team member.
- Members of the team celebrate my victories.
- Members of the team may well become my friends as well as my professional colleagues.

Appendix G

A Personal Leadership Conservation and Change Inventory

Doctoral study affords you the opportunity to assess your leadership ability and decide to conserve some leadership attitudes and behaviors while changing others. This process will take place in formal and informal settings. And, it is especially helpful to know where to turn when going through the challenge of changing leadership attitudes and behaviors.

What are three things about *my leadership* that I highly value and want to conserve?

What are the formal settings during doctoral study in which I will do this?

What are the informal settings during doctoral studies in which I will do this?

What are three things about *my leadership* that I want to change?

What are the formal settings during doctoral study in which I can take on the challenge of changing my leadership?

What are the informal settings during doctoral study in which I can work on changing my leadership?

Who in the doctoral program (fellow students, professors and others) can I turn to for help while taking on this challenge?

Appendix H

Identifying the Traits of Outstanding Leaders Encountered During My Doctoral Program

Doctoral study affords one with wonderful opportunities to experience outstanding leaders, some of whom are in the doctoral program and others who are guest speakers and the like. Please highlight the following qualities that you identified in experiencing their leadership:

_____   _____

Leader's Name   Leadership Position/Title

- Used applied intelligence (high-level common sense).
- Did his or her homework (facts + frameworks/context well in hand).
- An expert planner (left experience with concrete next steps in mind).
- Sense of purpose (vision) stated clearly and referred to when appropriate.
- Clearly committed to what needed to be done.
- Listened well and spoke to persons at their level of expertise.
- Came across as fair-minded.
- Authentic or genuine (not phony).
- Compassionate, empathetic (not patronizing), and sensitive.
- Not mean-spirited. Has a sense of humor.
- Willing to take risks (to make himself or herself vulnerable).
- Conveys sense of trust, or attitude that others can do what needs to be done.
- Able to bracket self (stand back) and look at self and situation with objectivity.
- Good of the organization a primary consideration, not simply self-absorbed.
- Able to build partnerships.

Appendix I

How Good and Comfortable are You as a Speaker and Listener

Doctoral study gives you an opportunity to assess and improve upon your speaking and listening skills. Please assess your comfort and proficiency on the following items, from 1 (low) to 5 (high). You may also have a trusted colleague and others assess your speaking and listening skills.

	Comfort	*Proficiency*
1. Speaking one-to-one	_____	_____
2. Listening one-to-one	_____	_____
3. Speaking to a small group	_____	_____
4. Listening in a small group	_____	_____
5. Answering questions after speaking to a small group	_____	_____
6. Speaking to a large group	_____	_____
7. Listening (as the speaker) to large group respondents	_____	_____
8. Answering questions after speaking to a large group	_____	_____
9. Telephone interviews	_____	_____
10. Television interviews	_____	_____
11. Radio interviews	_____	_____
12. Newspaper reporter interviews	_____	_____

A Conversation with Seymour B. Sarason about the Creation and Dynamics of the Dissertation Committee January 20, 2000

Dale Brubaker:	Seymour, I am curious as to your views on the creation and dynamics of the dissertation committee as a subject to be researched.
Seymour Sarason:	I could write a book on how and why over 45 years our Department of Psychology at Yale changed the rules, composition, and purposes of the committee because the previous type did not prevent serious rivalries *within* the committee *and* the department. And, of course, the students paid a high price!
Dale Brubaker:	It sounds as if you feel that this is indeed a subject that deserves researching and writing about.
Seymour Sarason:	Yes, the more I think about it the more convinced I am that you have come up with a subject which in all respects is an example of the creation of settings, the topic I explored in my 1988 book, *The Creation of Settings and the Future Societies*. Departments differ widely as to how and why they handle issues, and it would be fascinating to determine how that is related to the stated purposes of doing a dissertation.
Dale Brubaker:	Are there any other thoughts you have on this matter?
Seymour Sarason:	Yes, I have several stray thoughts:

- The student is the leader in that he or she is intent on finding out something new.
- The student seeks an advisor, someone who will be helpful and supportive.
- Advisors have a tendency to "take over" or in fact become the leader and since he or she has more power, the relationship can be very stressful and disappointing to the student.

- Then there is the committee and whatever "agreed-upon goals" of the student and advisor get challenged and transformed. Interpersonal rivalries, usually not articulated, are always in the picture.
- Is it any wonder that students have no stomach for research once they are through? It is like learning math.
- As the advisor, you have the responsibility to make students *feel safe* to talk. They have the responsibility to be revealing. What you and they have in common is the pursuit of truth, and it is that pursuit by which you judge outcomes.

Dale Brubaker:	Do I have your permission to share this conversation with my students and use it in my writing?
Seymour Sarason:	By all means, do so. I would like to be a fly on the wall of the seminar room when this is discussed.

Appendix K

The Dissertation Writer's Tool Box

1. Carefully read your university's Graduate School Catalogue as well as college, school, and department materials related to doctoral program and dissertation issues. These guidelines or "rules of the game" often have hidden messages that can be most helpful. For example, one university makes it clear that you don't have to have your doctoral program advisor as your dissertation advisor. Another university catalogue says that you can write your comprehensive examinations after three-fourths of your coursework is completed. This can be very useful in keeping your momentum so that you don't have a long pause between coursework and writing your comprehensive examinations.
2. Have a plan, such as the traditional dissertation outline, as a starting place after which you can work the plan. No matter what outline or format you choose to use, there will be elements of the traditional plan in your dissertation—for example, review of literature, methodology(ies), presentation of findings and analysis of findings. One good way to work the plan is to place a checkmark in front of the part of the plan you have used. This gives you confidence and inspiration to continue writing.
3. Work from outlines so that you don't wander into blind alleys. When finished writing at the end of a period of time, outline the next ideas you will write about, a tip from Hemingway. This helps you avoid start-up lag: feed the cat, get the paper, make coffee, twiddle your thumbs, and it's already noon.
4. Have a home base where you do your scholarly work. One student put crime-scene yellow tape from chair-to-chair at her dining room table to maintain her boundary.

5. Have other places where you are not interrupted in order to do your scholarly work. This affords variety and something different to look forward to from time to time. One student routinely visited a fast-food restaurant to do her proofreading. Another student used boring meetings to make lists to sharpen his writing: non-words, such as irregardless and doctorial; a second list of words that got on his nerves, such as impact as it reminded him of tooth-aches; a third list that identified words that needed to be looked up in the dictionary; and a final list of favorite words.

6. Avoid "hiding phrases," such as "I think," "it seems to me," "I feel," and the like. It is assumed that you think and feel and using such words steals your authority and power. For example, I think that my research findings suggest that . . . ," and "I feel that my research findings suggest that." "I believe" may be used judiciously to add emphasis but don't overuse it.

7. Use headings and sub headings where appropriate as this maps the writing for the reader. Write from an outline so that chapter title, headings, and subheadings fit together.

8. Be direct, rather than wandering around with your writing. Begin chapters and sections of chapters with topic sentences. For example, "The problem this study addresses is . . ." and "The purpose of this study is . . ."

9. Bring precision to your writing. Be concise; this is a creative act. Write clearly, simply, and consistently.

10. Avoid long paragraphs. Try to have paragraphs of no more than four to seven lines as they won't bore the reader and will have aesthetic appeal.

11. Anecdotes and examples add specific meaning to point you are making.

12. Header quotes (epigraphs) may be used to introduce chapters. They are often a good way to set the tone for the writing that follows.

13. Remember that reading is the soap and water of writing. Keep an eye out for potential dissertation topics and ideas as you write papers in classes. Ask yourself the question, "What problems need to be researched and written about?" Do the same thing as you read articles and books assigned in classes. Remember that these readings may well find their way into your comprehensive examinations and your dissertation's review of literature.

14. Give attention to research methodologies used by authors of the articles and books you read. Also do this in listening to speakers who come on campus or participate at conferences and conventions.

15. Work with your advisor to complete and file your program of study and dissertation prospectus. These are your contracts with the university and can be returned to if controversies arise. Changes in advisors and committee members often occur. Your written contracts stay. Keep your copies of these materials in a secure place.

16. Having a first-rate advisor, respected by committee members, is essential. Having a good relationship with your advisor is very important. Talk frankly with your advisor about the selection of committee members. Your committee has its own personality that may well be different from your relationships with individual faculty members. *Stay in touch with your advisor on a regular basis. Give regular progress reports to her/him.*

17. Give attention to the research and writing of your advisor and committee members. This will give you a good idea of what they value.

18. All students need a copy editor, not simply a proofreader. A copy editor doesn't simply read to find spelling errors and the like. A first-rate copy editor also reads for clarity of ideas, sentence structure, paragraph construction, and good word choice. Failure to have a first-rate copy editor can annoy the readers (committee members) and, if numerous, become a major problem.

19. Many problems are of an organizational nature. The lack of a conceptual framework that holds together is a real issue. A conceptual framework is a map that will help the reader know where you, the dissertation writer, are going. Failure to have a schedule or calendar for what is to be done and when is another major issue. Go through your preliminary calendar with your advisor that can be revised through discussion to set realistic goals.

20. Interpretation of findings, usually the chapter that follows presentation of findings, is frequently the most difficult part of writing a dissertation.

21. The review of literature chapter must be focused, research-based rather than simply experience-based. You must demonstrate that you can make sense out of the research that you cite. Use quotes if you want to convey the original meaning in the words of the original author(s).

22. Conveying your passion for the subject is essential and a key motivator. It will let committee members know that you are not simply jumping hurdles to get a degree. Passion for the subject will demonstrate that you intend to make a difference with your writing and it will give you personal meaning.

23. Be alert to the pitfall of over-promising in your chapter on findings or results.

24. Clearly define terms and *anchor them in the literature.*

Appendix L

Example of a Traditional Table of Contents for a Dissertation

Tables of contents for dissertations vary a good deal. The decision as to the format for your dissertation is in the hands of you, your advisor, and your committee. Because doctoral students frequently ask us what a "typical" table of contents looks like, we have included the following somewhat traditional example.

Title

Subtitle

Brief Autobiographical Sketch (optional, requested by some advisors to treat factors that led you to doing this research and writing)

Approval Page (lines for signatures by your advisor and committee members)

Acknowledgements (thanks to those who helped—names and positions usually given)

Chapter 1	*Introduction* (written in future, will-do tense)
	Purpose of the study (importance and timeliness of subject highlighted)
	Need for the study (how your study will add to the literature)
	The contextual problem (problem in the larger context)
	The research problem
	Methodology (sets the stage for Chapter 3—includes specific research hypotheses and/or questions to be addressed throughout the dissertation with identification and rationale for research methodology(ies) highlighted)
	Definitions (key terms in title and subtitle usually defined plus other important terms)
	Overview of the remainder of the dissertation

Chapter 2   *Review of the Literature*
               Introduction (indicates why this review is important and not
               simply filler)
               Key indicators (themes) used in computer search serve as orga-
               nizing concepts
Chapter 3   *Methodology*
               Describe why methodology(ies) chosen with this rationale
               in greater depth in contrast to brief description in Chapter 1
               (particulars are part of larger research design spelled out in the
               present chapter)
Chapter 4   *Presentation of Findings*
Chapter 5   *Analysis of Findings*
Chapter 6   *Summary Conclusions and Recommendations*
               First part of this chapter like Chapter 1 but now in the past tense
               Two kinds of recommendations: for further study and
               programmatic

Appendix M

Giving your Dissertation a Title and Subtitle in Relation to the Definitions Section of the Dissertation

You have now identified a research topic. Over the course of your dissertation research and writing, you may change the title and subtitle several times. You are probably wise to have a list of each title and subtitle plus the date when you chose it. This will be a good running record of your dissertation research and writing. With this in mind, have a first go at giving your dissertation a title and subtitle. (You may discover as you move forward that you wish to delete the subtitle.)

Title

Subtitle

The key terms in your title and subtitle will need to be defined. This can be one of the most difficult challenges you will face. It is a section of the dissertation that demands precision.

First, what are the key terms that must be defined? Second, what definition for each term will serve you best? You will note that wherever possible, the term's definition should be referenced in the literature and/or dictionary. Third, the definitions you reference will probably need to be fleshed out some in order to give the reader a more complete understanding of the terms.

The following two examples serve as cautionary tales as students had to revise their dissertations because of problems with inadequate or missing definitions. Committee members defined *curriculum* as a course of study. The dissertation writer defined *curriculum* as what students experience, with the course of study simply serving as a springboard that is only *a part* of what emerges in students' experience and learning. The student's advisor suggested that the student put CURRICLUM, as he defined it, in caps and curriculum, as the committee defined it, in lower case. The committee agreed with the advisor's suggestion. The reader was alerted at the time this key term first appeared in the dissertation as to this distinction.

In another situation, the doctoral student defined *charisma* as a divinely conferred gift or power used by leaders to realize positive organizational goals. At the dissertation prospectus meeting, a committee member said that *charisma* is a kind of emotional power that can influence others for good or evil purposes, with Hitler and Stalin cited as examples of this. This committee member and two other colleagues said that they had never heard of the student's definition of charisma. The dissertation advisor excused herself for a moment and returned to the defense with a dictionary that revealed both definitions of charisma were listed. The committee agreed that the doctoral student needed to address this issue in a separate definitions section of Chapter 1, the place where the stage would be set for how the student was using the term in the dissertation.

The doctoral student turned to the definitive book on definitions in education, Israel Scheffler's *The Language of Education* (Springfield, IL: Charles Thomas, 1960). Scheffler identifies three kinds of definitions: (1) *descriptive* (explanatory—reference to accepted prior usage as in "A tree is a tree."); (2) *stipulative* (communicatory—designed to facilitate discussion as in "When I say education, I mean schooling..."); and (3) *prescriptive/programmatic* (moral—non-negotiable as in "This researcher uses charisma to mean "a divinely conferred gift or power used by leaders to realize positive organizational goals" and benchmarks as "a standard in assessing student progress in the *No Child Left Behind* program").

The point of all of this is that words in general and definitions in particular are extremely important in dissertation research and writing and the scholar must bring precision to this matter.

Appendix N

Trouble Shooting the Dissertation

John A. Hattie, Professor of Education at the University of Auckland, New Zealand and renowned researcher writes: "Too many students complete their thesis or dissertation and say 'If only I had known X'" (2007, p. 2).

In order to find out how doctoral graduates looked back at their own dissertation experiences, we conducted a series of interviews with one primary question in mind: "What do you wish you had known to avoid or correct the problems you encountered in doing a dissertation?" We also drew on our experiences in advising doctoral students and working with dissertation committees to answer this question.

Doctoral graduates' comments and appropriate references to a key resource, *Theses and Dissertations: A Guide to Planning, Research, and Writing* (Thomas & Brubaker, 2008) are given.

1. The Validity Question. "I simply wasn't prepared for a critical remark made by a professor after reading my work: 'How do you establish the validity of your qualitative research methodology?' I basically had three choices: (1) the question isn't appropriate given the kind of research I did; (2) the question is appropriate and there are terms *within the qualitative research literature* that will help me answer your question; or (3) the question is a good one and there are terms *within the quantitative research literature* that are transferable to qualitative research methodology. [See Chapter 14, "Mounting a Persuasive Defense," in *Theses and Dissertations* (T & D).]

2. Shattered Expectations. "I chose this dissertation topic because of my passion for the subject and my 'at risk' students. But when my data came in it turned out all wrong. I couldn't use the study to make the case for my

treatment—the reform effort in which I had invested so many resources. I was forced to examine my role as a scholar and my role as an activist on the firing line." [See Chapter 9, "Things That Go Wrong," in T & D.]

3. Professional Disagreements. "I had no idea when I began this process how much my success in researching and writing a dissertation would depend on the personalities of my committee members. Having the right advisor was essential, but this didn't assure me that anyone else would approve my work. I could make a list as long as my arm as to interpersonal conflicts that had to be avoided or faced." [See Chapter 9, "Things That Go Wrong," in T & D.]

4. Searching the Literature. "At first I thought the review of literature chapter would be the easiest chapter to write. In the dissertations I read, this chapter appeared to be 'filler.' But my advisor had other things in mind. She wanted this chapter to have integrity, by which she meant it should fit or be an integral part of the whole dissertation. My challenge was to know what to look for, have system for recording, it and connecting it, with the rest of the dissertation." [See Chapter 3, "Searching the Literature," in T & D.]

5. Stating the Research Problem. "One of the first mistakes I made in organizing my dissertation was to confuse the research problem with the general problem in society my study addressed. I wanted to 'solve' the problem of poverty in low socio-economic schools in the district where I work but my research problem was narrower than that, and something to researched rather than directly addressed as a societal problem. This also had implications for the recommendations section at the end of my dissertation. I had to make a distinction between recommendations for further study and recommendations for programmatic changes in the schools. [See Chapter 4, "Sources and Types of Research Problems" and Chapter 6, "Stating the Problem and Its Rationale" in T & D.]

6. Changing My Topic. "I lost interest in my first topic but thought I could put myself on automatic pilot and finish my project. Then I heard a lecture that helped me identify a topic for which I had a real passion. As I look back, I wish I had known the specific steps I should have taken at this point. I needed an efficient plan to know what to do and who to involve." [See Chapter 2, "Sources of Guidance," in T & D.]

7. Definitions. "I hit a real snag at the point when I thought my writing was done. A committee member pointed out that I was using the term 'education' in a narrow way by only referring to formal education in classrooms. She asked me, in fact directed me, to add a section on definitions in Chapter 1 with an introductory sentence saying that these definitions

will be used consistently throughout the dissertation." [See Chapter 6, "Stating the Problem and Its Rationale," in T & D.]

8. Collecting and Organizing Information. "Once I had chosen my topic I began collecting information from every conceivable source. I truly reached the point of information overload. What I should have had were good systems for organizing information as I collected it." [See Chapter 3, "Searching the Literature," Chapter 7, "Types of Research Methods and Sources of Information," Chapter 8, "Data Collection Techniques and Instruments," Chapter 10, "Classification Patterns," and Chapter 11, "Summarizing Information Verbally, Numerically, and Graphically" in T & D.]

9. Interpreting Information. "The next to last chapter of the dissertation was the most difficult to write. My challenge was to describe the meanings I found in the information I had collected. 'Hermeneutics' was a concept I had studied in several of my courses, and so I used it to introduce this chapter. What I needed but didn't have was a system for classifying different kinds of interpretation. [See Chapter 12, "Modes of Interpretation," in T & D.]

10. Reaching a Wider Audience. "When I finished my dissertation I had two feelings—elation and emptiness. I felt academically successful and wondered, 'Is there life after doing a dissertation?' My advisor suggested that I write and get published articles from my dissertation, but I didn't know what specific steps to take." [See Chapter 15, "Reaching a Wider Audience," in T & D.]

Appendix O

The Case for Reflective Action in Dissertation Writing

Each of us constructs a worldview, a sense of self in relation to the world, and dissertation research and writing reflects the worldview of the doctoral student. In fact, dissertation research and writing is an excellent time and place in a person's life to get in touch with one's worldview and hone it. It is a stage of life when the doctoral student searches for meaning and purpose in order to sharpen one's vision or map of the territory. This map of the territory is in its simplest sense a theory. When doctoral students share worldviews with each other a reciprocity of perspectives is the result.

Praxis, reflective action, is the process the doctoral students goes through in order to shape and hone dissertations. A love for learning is the centerpiece of this journey. What are the key elements of this learning process?

- Curiosity is a driving force that intensifies life and helps us continue to have a passion for the subject of our research and writing.
- Being honest and authentic about what we know and don't know helps us avoid the erosion and waste of resources associated with trying to keep up a false front. This will not only lend a "ring of truth" to our writing but will give us personal satisfaction as we celebrate what we learn.
- A playfulness in relating to ideas will lead us to amusing surprises that entertain us and stimulate our sense of humor, thus keeping us from taking ourselves too seriously.
- Sharing what we learn in doing research and writing, the application of what we've learned, will give us the feeling that we are helping create a better world—even to the extent that we are occasionally embarrassingly enthusiastic.

- In doing our research and writing, we will experience the joy of translating what we learn for others in an understandable way.
- In serving as a learning guide for others, we will help them discover talents in themselves that they didn't know they have.
- And finally, we will recognize and reward many different kinds of intelligence in ourselves and others—a celebration of differences.

Appendix P

Note Taking as an Important Part of the Research and Writing Process

Collecting and recording ideas is an important first step in the research and writing process. Note taking is one way to participate in this process. As a doctoral student you will be in a variety of learning activities where note-taking can take place. You will listen to speakers on campus and off-campus. Examples of the latter are conferences and conventions. You will also have access to a variety of media, audio and visual, that can be an important source of information. You may use electronic devices and paper, such as note cards, to take notes. The following guidelines should be helpful as you take notes.

- When taking notes you will bring to this process an "anticipatory set"—a set of attitudes and predispositions as to the importance of what you are doing. What you are looking for and recording will be seen through your ideas and may differ considerably from others' views of the same situation. In other words, modes of interpretation are unique. Your goals and background knowledge will influence what you record.
- Notes should reflect insofar as possible the original meaning intended by the owner of the information.
- Be sure to distinguish between paraphrases and quotes. Be sure to reference quotes in reading materials with page numbers. Also reference paraphrases in reading materials with page numbers in the event that you wish to return for quoting purposes.
- You may return to notes taken to rewrite them in more legible form. It is also useful to sort or categorize notes according to common themes. Important points may also be highlighted.
- Give careful thought to where your notes might fit into a dissertation, article, monograph or book. You may write notes on your notes to follow

this advice. For example, USE THIS IN REVIEW OF LITERATURE CHAPTER. Leave room in the right margins for such notes and key concepts you have identified.

- You will be challenged to use a discerning ear and eye in the note-taking process. Speakers will often establish a tone in their presentations.
- It is often helpful to draw a picture of the setting in which you take notes. For example, locate where the speaker stands, where windows and doors are located, the seating arrangement, and so on. This graphic picture will return you to the setting when you view it in the future, once again remind you of the sound of the situation.
- For further ideas on note taking, see Chapter 3, "Searching the Literature," pp. 31–46 and Chapter 8, "Data Collection Techniques and Instruments," and Chapter 10, "Classification Patterns," in R.M. Thomas and Dale L. Brubaker, *Theses and Dissertations: A Guide to Planning Research and Writing* (Thousand Oaks, Ca: Corwin Press).

Appendix Q

Checklist for Shaping and/or Refining Your Dissertation

Please check those items that you are satisfied you can do or have done well. At the end of each item is a reference to the place in *Theses and Dissertations: A Guide to Planning, Research and Writing* (T & D) by Thomas, R.M. and Brubaker, D.L. (Thousand Oaks, CA: Corwin Press, 2007) where you can get information you need in order to place a check in front of the item.

1. I can clearly state the function of the literature review in my dissertation project in order to introduce this chapter. [Chapter 3 in T & D.]
2. I have a concise and precise system for coding materials from the literature. [Chapter 3 in T & D.]
3. I am able to identify criteria for distinguishing between a good topic and a bad one. [Chapter 4 in T & D.]
4. I can identify the two most popular ways to stage a research problem. [Chapter 6 in T & D.]
5. I know where the basic terms to be defined in Chapter 1 of the dissertation are located. [Chapter 6 in T & D.]
6. I can list the different ways that researchers define key terms. [Chapter 6 in T & D.]
7. I am clear as to the distinction between the contextual problem and the research problem and can state this difference. [Chapter 6 in T & D.]
8. I can define and state the advantages of case study research. [Chapter 7 in T & D.]
9. I can clearly explain how research methods are matched with research questions. [Chapter 7 in T & D.]
10. I can describe several ways/kinds of observational research. [Chapter 8 in T & D.]

11. I can identify and explain alternative interview strategies. [Chapter 8 in T & D.]
12. I can define and describe several types of questionnaire items. [Chapter 8 in T & D.]
13. I can describe the functions and sources of tests. [Chapter 8 in T & D.]
14. I can define and discuss classifying and summarizing information—two ways of organizing information. [Chapters 10 & 11 in T & D.]
15. I am clear as to the role of interpretation in relation to my research questions as well as the meaning of *hermeneutics.* [Chapter 12 in T & D.]
16. I can identify and execute guidelines for the writing of the final version of the dissertation. [Chapter 13 in T & D.]
17. I am prepared to answer "the validity question" if asked to do so by a member of my committee. [Chapter 14 in T & D.]
18. When through writing my dissertation, I will know the concrete next steps to take in reaching a wider audience.
19. I am familiar with and prepared to do internet publishing. [Chapter 15 in T & D.]
20. I have an outline of a dissertation proposal that gives me a good idea as to how to begin writing the dissertation. [Appendix at the end of T & D.]

References

Achilles, C.M. & Brewer, E.W. (2008). *Finding funding: Grant writing from start to finish, including project management and internet use* (5th ed.). Thousand Oaks, CA: Corwin Press.

Adams, J.G. (1983). *Without precedent.* New York: Horton.

Angelou, M. (2009, Dec. 7). The take. *Newsweek,* 27.

Archer, J. (2007, March 14). National network aims to recraft Ed.D. for practitioners. *Education Week,* 7.

Brubaker, D. (1982). *Curriculum planning: The dynamics of theory and practice.* Glenview, Illinois: Scott, Foresman and Company.

Brubaker, D. (2004). *Revitalizing curriculum leadership: Inspiring and empowering your school community* (2nd ed.). Thousand Oaks, CA: Corwin Press.

Brubaker, D.. & Coble, L.D. (2005). *The hidden leader: Leadership lessons on the potential within.* Thousand Oaks, CA: Corwin Press.

Brubaker, D. (2006). *The charismatic leader: The presentation of self and the creation of educational settings.* Thousand Oaks, CA: Corwin Press.

Brubaker, D. (2010, August). Cherishing the memory of Seymour Sarason— Public intellectual, mentor and friend. *Mentoring & Tutoring: Partnership in Learning, 18* (3), 313–7.

Brubaker, D. & Williams, M. (2010). *Why the Principalship? Making the Leap from the Classroom.* Lanham, MD: Rowman & Littlefield.

Buckley, R. (2010). *This business of writing...Wresting order out of chaos.* Camden, SC: P.E.N. Press.

Burns, D.D. (2009). *Feeling good. The new mood therapy.* New York: Harper.

Cavell, L.J. (2000). Graduation student unionization in higher education. *ERIC Digest.* http://ericdigests.org/2001-3/graduate.htm, 1–6.

Chittister, J. (2008). *The gift of years: Growing older gracefully.* New York: BlueBridge.

Cohen, P. (2010, August 24). Scholars test web alternative to the venerable peer review. *New York Times,* 1, 3.

Conroy, P. (2002). *My losing season.* Garden City, NJ: Doubleday.

Gladwell, M. (2008). *Outliers: The story of success.* New York: Doubleday Anchor.

Glatthorn, A.A. (2002). *Publish or perish: The educator's imperative.* Thousand Oaks, CA: Corwin Press.

Goffman, E. (1959). The *presentation of self in everyday life.* New York: Doubleday Anchor.

Goodman, R. (September 4, 2010). *Doctoral graduate interview.*

Graham, H.D. (2010, June 5). Should we abolish ranking universities by their reputations? *Vanderbilt Register,* http://www.vanderbilt.edu/News/register/Jun5_00/story12html 1–5.

Graham, H.D. & Diamond, N. (1997). *The rise of American research universities: Elites and challengers in the postwar era.* Baltimore: Johns Hopkins University Press.

Hattie, J.A. (2008). Endorsement in a flyer for Thomas, R.M. & Brubaker, D.L. (2008). *Theses and dissertations: A guide to planning, research and writing.* Thousand Oaks, CA: Corwin Press.

Jung, C.G. (1973). *Collected works of C.G. Jung* (2nd ed.). Bollingen Ser., No. 20 (Princeton, N.J.: Princeton University Press, 1973), trans. R.F.C. Hull, Vol. II, *Psychology and religion*: West and East, 75., as cited in Peck, p. 17.

Kidder, T. (2006). *My detachment: A memoir.* New York: Random House.

Levinson, D. (1985). *The seasons of a man's life.* New York: Alfred A. Knopf.

Levinson, D. (1996). *The seasons of a woman's life.* New York: Alfred A. Knopf.

Linver, S. (1978). *Speakeasy.* New York: Summit.

Lopez, S. (2008). *The soloist: A lost dream, an unlikely friendship, and the redemptive power of music.* New York: Berkley Books.

Macdonald. J.B. (1977, December). Interview conducted by Ruth Fairfield at the University of North Carolina at Greensboro.

McCourt, F. (2005). *Teacher man.* New York: Scribner.

Mitchell, A. (2005). *Talking back.* New York: Viking.

Mortenson, G. (2009). *Stones into schools: Promoting peace with books, not bombs in Afghanistan and Pakistan.* New York: Viking.

Nettles, M.T. & Millet, C.M. (2006). *Three magic letters: Getting to Ph.D.* Baltimore, MD: The Johns Hopkins University Press.

Nouwen, H. (1986). *Reaching out: The three movements of the spiritual life.* New York: Doubleday.

Nouwen, H. (2006). *Spiritual direction.* New York: Harper-Collins.

Peck, M.S. (1978). *The road less traveled: A new psychology of love, traditional values and spiritual growth.* New York: Simon & Schuster.

Peterson, S.M., Valk, Constance, Baker, A.C., Brugger, L. & Hightower, A.D. (2010, May). *Mentoring & Tutoring: Partnership in Learning, 18* (2), 155–75.

Ramo, J.C. (2009). *The age of the unthinkable: Why the new world disorder constantly surprises us and what we can do about it.* New York: Little, Brown & Co.

Sarason, S.B. (1972). *The creation of educational settings and the future societies.* San Francisco: Jossey-Bass.

Sarason, S.B. (1988). *The making of an American psychologist.* San Francisco: Jossey-Bass.

Sarason, S.B. (2002). *Educational reform: A self-scrutinizing memoir.* San Francisco: Jossey-Bass.

Scheffler, I. (1960). *The language of education.* Springfield, IL: Charles Thomas.

Schlesinger, A., Jr. (2000). *Journals: 1952–2000.* New York: The Penguin Press.

Senge, P. (1990). *The fifth discipline: The art and practice of the learning organization.* New York: Doubleday.

Shapiro, H.S. (2010, August). David Purpel, emeritus professor: In memoriam. *Mentoring & Tutoring: Partnership in Learning, 18* (3), 319–20.

Shure, L. (September 4, 2010). *Doctoral graduate interview.*

Simon, L.H. (December 18, 2010). *Doctoral graduate interview.*

Steinem, G. (1992). *Revolution from within: A book of self-esteem.* New York: Little, Brown.

Thomas, R.M. & Brubaker, D.L. (2001). *Avoiding thesis and dissertation pitfalls: 61 cases of problems and solutions.* Westport, CT: Bergin & Garvey.

Thomas, R.M. & Brubaker, D.L. (2008). *Theses and dissertations: A guide to planning, research and writing* (2nd ed.). Thousand Oaks, CA: Corwin Press.

Tyler, R. (1949). *Basic principles of curriculum and instruction.* Chicago: The University Of Chicago Press.

Vanslyke-Briggs, K. (2010). *The nurturing teacher: Managing the stress of caring.* Lanham, MD: Rowman & Littlefield.

Webster's New World Compact Desk Dictionary and Style Guide (2002, 2nd ed.). Cleveland, Ohio: Wiley Publishing, Inc.

Zahorik, J.A. & Brubaker, D.L. (1972). *Toward more humanistic instruction.* Dubuque, Iowa: Wm. Brown.

Index

About the Authors

Michael D. Brubaker is an Assistant Professor and Academic Coordinator of the Substance Abuse Counseling Program in the School of Human Services in the College of Education, Criminal Justice, and Human Services at the University of Cincinnati. He received his Ph.D. in Mental Health Counseling from the University of Florida, his M.S. in Professional Counseling from Georgia State University, his M.Div. from Emory University, and his B.S. in Business Administration from the University of North Carolina at Chapel Hill. As a licensed chemical dependency counselor and a Nationally Certified Counselor, he has served many populations in the roles of clinician, administrator, researcher, and professor throughout his career. His current research addresses the clinical and social barriers to substance abuse and mental health services for various underserved populations.

Dale L. Brubaker is Professor Emeritus of Educational Leadership and Cultural Studies at the University of North Carolina at Greensboro. He has also served on the faculties of the University of California-Santa Barbara and the University of Wisconsin-Milwaukee. He received his Ph.D. and M.A. in Education from Michigan State University and his B.A. from Albion College. He is the author or coauthor of numerous books on educational leadership, curriculum and dissertation research and writing, including *The Charismatic Leader: The Presentation of Self and the Creation of Educational Settings, Revitalizing Curriculum Leadership; Inspiring and Empowering Your School Community, Theses and Dissertations: A Guide to Planning Research, and Writing* (with R. Murray Thomas), and *Avoiding Thesis and Dissertation Pitfalls* (with R. Murray Thomas).